IMPACT PRICING

Sarah,
Make an Impact!
MS

IMPACT PRICING
Your Blueprint for Driving Profits

Mark Stiving
PragmaticPricing.com

Publisher: Jere Calmes
Cover Design: Andrew Welyczko, CWL Publishing Enterprises, Inc.
Editorial and Production Services: CWL Publishing Enterprises, Inc., Madison, Wisconsin, www.cwlpub.com

Copyright © 2011 by Mark A. Stiving. All rights reserved.

Reproduction of any part of this work beyond that permitted by Section 107 or 108 of the 1976 United States Copyright Act without the express permission of the copyright owner is unlawful. Requests for permission or further information should be addressed to the Business Products Division, Entrepreneur Media, Inc.

This publication is designed to provide accurate and authoritative information in regard to the subject matter covered. It is sold with the understanding that the publisher is not engaged in rendering legal, accounting, or other professional services. If legal advice or other expert assistance is required, the services of a competent professional person should be sought.
—From a Declaration of Principles jointly adopted by a Committee of the American Bar Association and a Committee of Publishers and Associations

ISBN 13: 978-1-59918-431-9
10: 1-59918-431-1

15 14 13 12 11   10 9 8 7 6 5 4 3 2 1

**For Carol
(and True Love)**

Contents

Preface · xi

Part One. Pricing Fundamentals: What You Need to Know · 1

1. Vision: See Where Your Pricing Needs to Go · 3
Strategy Is a Communication Tool · 4
Market Cap Pricing · 6
Nonfinancial Objectives · 10
Low Price as a Corporate Strategy: Don't Do It! · 11
Summary · 14

2. Pricing Strategies: A First Glance · 17
Neutral, Penetration, and Skimming · 18
Value-Based Pricing · 21
Negotiated vs. TIOLI Pricing · 22
Summary · 24

3. Value: What Is Your Product Worth? · 27
Customers Buy Perceived Value · 28
Choice Value, Value in Use, and Deal Value · 31
Will I? Which One? · 33
Your Customer's Brain: Value-Based Buying · 38
Summary · 39

Contents

4. Value-Based Pricing: Mandatory to Maximize Profits — 41
   Value Accounting — 42
   Identify Your Customer's Second-Best Option — 45
   Determine the Price of the Second-Best Option — 46
   List Your Advantages and Disadvantages Relative to the Second-Best Option — 47
   Estimate in Dollars the Value of Each Advantage and Disadvantage — 49
   Calculate Your Price — 50
   Summary — 51

5. Create Value: Let Pricing Guide You — 53
   Create Real Value with Differentiation — 54
   Increase Perceived Value — 56
   Influence the Second-Best Option — 58
   Influence the Perceived Price of the Second-Best Option — 60
   Use Price to Signal Quality — 60
   Summary — 62

6. Costs Matter: But Not How You Think — 65
   Fixed Costs Are Irrelevant to Pricing — 66
   Variable Costs Are Relevant — 68
   Standard Costs Can Be a Mistake — 70
   Observable Costs — 72
   Cost-Plus Pricing — 73
   Summary — 74

Part Two. Pricing Segmentation: The Most Profitable Strategies — 77

7. Introduction to Price Segmentation: Rich and Poor — 79
   How to Segment on Price — 81
   Is This Fair? — 82
   Summary — 84

8. Customer Characteristics: Who Are You? — 87
   Age — 88
   Local vs. Tourist — 88
   Geography — 89
   Market Segment — 89

Contents

    Historical Purchase Behavior   89
    Summary   90

9. Customer Behaviors: Jump This Hurdle   **93**
    Coupons (Effort)   94
    Rebates (Effort)   95
    Sales Events (Patience)   95
    End-Aisle Displays (Thoroughness)   96
    Purchase Ahead (Foresight)   97
    Loyalty Clubs (Investment)   97
    Channel/Internet   97
    Pay as You Wish   98
    Summary   99

10. Transaction Characteristics: At Point of Purchase   **101**
    Volume   102
    Weather   103
    Time of Day   104
    Location   104
    First-Time Buyer   104
    Number of Quotes   105
    Summary   105

11. Loyalty and Price Segmentation: Treat Your Best Customers the Best   **107**

Part Three. Portfolio Pricing: No Product Is an Island   **111**

12. Versioning: Develop the Right Product Line   **113**
    Versioning   114
    Good, Better, Better ...   116
    Good, Better, Best   121
    Version by Market   122
    Summary   123

13. Complementary Products: Linking and Leveraging   **125**
    Loss Leader   126
    Durables and Consumables   127
    Accessories   128
    Captive Customers   128
    De-Bundling   129
    Bundling   130

Contents

Product Funnel	132
Summary	133
14. Free: How to Get Paid for Free	**135**
Summary	140

Part Four. Pricing Dynamics: Prepare for Change — 141

15. Introduction to Pricing Dynamics: Customer Expectations	**143**
Customers Despise Price Increases	144
Start High, Then Discount	145
EDLP vs. Hi-Lo	148
Summary	149
16. Responding to the Economy: The 800-Pound Gorilla	**151**
Recessions	152
Inflation	153
Summary	155
17. Responding to Competitors: Darn Them	**157**
Price Wars	159
Summary	162
18. Product Life Cycle: Prices Change with Age	**163**
New Product Introduction	164
Growth	165
Maturity	166
Decline	166
Portfolio	167
Summary	168
Wrap Up: Now What?	**169**
Pricing Drives Products	170
Is Your Pricing Right?	171
How This Book Was Priced	172
How This Book Was Priced	**173**
Glossary	**175**
Bibliography	**183**
Index	**185**

Preface

The single most important decision in evaluating a business is pricing power.

—Warren Buffett

Price is the most powerful marketing tool. To have a real impact on your profitability, you swing the sledgehammer called pricing. Even though it's the most powerful, it's also the least understood.

You already know pricing is important. That's why you picked up this book. Your burning question is how to do it better. How can you use this sledgehammer to increase your profits?

A pricing expert would certainly be able to find areas to improve your pricing. This isn't a knock on you because it is true for almost every company. The real question is: Can you do this yourself? Can you, without hiring a specialist, find ways to improve your pricing that significantly impact your profitability? That's the goal of this book, to provide you with

Preface

a roadmap on how to find new pricing strategies to increase your profits.

Most books on pricing describe tens, hundreds, and maybe thousands of pricing strategies and tactics. Which ones work for you? Unfortunately, it's not easy to answer that question in a book. Instead of attempting to identify the specific tactics that will work for you, this book breaks down pricing into the big-picture concepts that significantly impact profitability in almost every company. The objective is to help you focus on the areas where you are likely to find gold.

I once interviewed an athlete active in ski jumping, the sport where a skier goes straight down a ramp and when he reaches the end, he jumps and flies through the air as far as possible. I still recall what he thought was one of the hardest skills required to be a good ski jumper—telescoping focus. "While going down the ramp you need a broad focus, looking for issues in the snow, feeling changes in the wind, anything that might influence the jump. As you approach the end of the ramp, you have to narrow your focus, intently watching the edge to get the timing of the jump just right. Once you leave the ramp, you need a wide focus again during flight, and then narrow your focus once more for the landing."

Pricing, like ski jumping, requires telescoping focus. It needs both a broad focus and a narrow focus. However, most people who work in pricing have a narrow focus, figuring out how to put a specific price on a specific product, executing whatever pricing strategies and processes have been handed to them.

Somebody in your company needs a telescoping focus on pricing ... and that is you. This book will guide you in your quest. The ski jumper's broad focus had him looking for changes in snow or wind and once he identified an area of

Preface

concern, he dealt with it. This book will show you the broad areas in pricing where you should most be concerned. Then, as you drill down deeper, with increasing focus, you'll create new pricing strategies that grow your profits.

> Somebody in your company needs a telescoping focus on pricing... and that is you.

#impactpricing

The pricing framework you'll learn will help you impact your company's performance. This book begins with some fundamentals you must know before jumping into setting pricing strategies. Don't shortchange the process. Be sure to read the fundamentals. The book then launches into many profitable strategies you'll want to use in your company. These powerful strategies are presented broadly with specific examples to help you apply this strategy to your situation. As you know, pricing is different for almost every product and market, but the broad strategies presented here are universal. After reading this book, you'll know where to find the most additional profit to be gained through pricing.

B2B vs. B2C

We are all familiar with B2C (business to consumer) markets because we are all consumers. We purchase gas at Chevron or groceries at Kroger. We purchase books from Amazon.com or our local bookstores. We buy hamburgers and fries from McDonald's. All of these are B2C markets, and we are all familiar at least with the buying side of these markets.

However, you may be less familiar with B2B (business to business) markets. These are the oil refineries that sell gasoline to the Chevron stations. They are the parts manufacturers that sell car parts to Ford. Companies like Cisco, SAP, Oracle, Intel, Flextronics, and McKinsey are all companies that sell mostly to other companies.

Preface

There are differences between B2B and B2C markets that are relevant to pricing. For example, consumers tend to be more susceptible to psychological aspects of pricing than professional buyers at corporations. And in chapter 2 you will read more about negotiated vs. TIOLI (take it or leave it) markets. However, the key pricing strategies covered in this book apply to both B2B and B2C markets. Regardless of which type of industry you are in, you'll want to know these concepts.

This book uses a lot of pricing examples. Most of them are from B2C markets because these examples are familiar to more people. As pointed out earlier, most of us buy gas, groceries, books, haircuts, and more. Far fewer of us are familiar with SalesForce.com, the market for buying bulk paper, or the management consulting industry. As much as possible this book will use examples from B2C markets so more people can relate while still learning the important pricing strategy being discussed. Although the examples are mostly B2C, the concepts and strategies apply equally well in B2B markets.

Whichever market you are in, this book is for you.

Definition of Product

The term *product* is used throughout the book to mean what the company is selling. Product may be a physical product, like a shovel, or it may be a service, like a haircut, or it may be software like Microsoft Excel. Product may even be a bundle of some or all of these. The word *product* is used as a shortcut to avoid saying "product and/or services" all the time. This term *product* also means the entire offering, including any warranties, packaging, services, customer support, technical support—everything except price.

Preface

An Overview of This Book

All pricing situations are different. B2B differs from B2C, physical products differ from services and software, durables differ from consumables, and so on. Yet there are pricing truths, concepts, and strategies that span the differences in these markets. When you focus narrowly on the details, each of these is different. But when you look at the broad focus, they all benefit from similar pricing strategies. These broad focus areas are value, segmentation, portfolio, and pricing dynamics. Each is tackled in its own part of the book.

The book is divided into four parts.

Part One: Pricing Fundamentals—This critical part teaches you how to think about strategy, value, and costs. These key concepts are used throughout the remainder of the book.

Part Two: Price Segmentation—Once you know how a customer values your product, this section describes how to get different customers to purchase at prices closer to their actual willingness to pay.

Part Three: Portfolio Pricing—If you have more than one product, you have the opportunity to make more profit by pricing the portfolio intelligently, taking into account the relationships among products. If you don't have more than one product you will learn why you should.

Part Four: Pricing Dynamics—Things change. Your costs change. Your competitors' prices change. The economy changes. Your prices must change, too. This section helps you think through and plan for your inevitable price changes.

To make the most efficient use of your time while having a real impact on your pricing, each chapter is organized into four sections:

Key concepts—Bullet points of important concepts you will know after reading the chapter.

Preface

Main text

Summary questions—A series of questions for you to answer that help you think through the application of some of the techniques to your business.

Action box—A blank space for you to write down what you are going to do.

Hashtags—Near the sidebars throughout the text, you'll find a Twitter hashtag (#impactpricing). This is a reminder that you may want to do a Twitter search on material in that sidebar.

Pricing is the most powerful and least understood marketing tool. It is time to harness the power. It is time to have an IMPACT.

Acknowledgments

Writing a first book is fun, hard, frustrating, enlightening, boring, challenging, lonely, scary, and, at the end, fulfilling. Many people deserve thanks for supporting, challenging, encouraging, and just plain helping me.

Rupert Hart, author of *Recession Storming*, is the impetus behind this book. He convinced me that I could write one and mentored me through the process.

This book is much better because of the debates every Sunday night with the ping-pong crew. Brent Bilger and Morgan Littlewood always provide valuable insight and perspective, even though they seemed to get too much enjoyment finding my mistakes. Cameron Bilger has been extremely supportive, reading early drafts and providing needed feedback.

Many owners of small companies have allowed me to work with them, using pricing concepts to improve their businesses. Every engagement has something new to teach. I especially want to thank Russell Barnett, Blanca Pradenas, Frank White, Diane Lees, Brian Jenks, and Peter Long.

I want to thank Toastmasters International. In the three years I've been involved with this organization, they have taught me to communicate clearly, follow my dreams, and keep moving forward. Special thanks go to Warren Riley, Miriam Kojnok, John Love, Grace Murao, Vern McGeorge, Henry Miller, Birgit Starmanns, and Mike Barsul.

The World Champions EDGE turned my dream into a vision. They provided the insight into what is possible. Here is a huge thank you to Darren LaCroix and Craig Valentine. They are my role models.

Finally, my wife, Carol, is an angel. She was loving and supportive even while I spent hours and hours typing away on my computer.

Thank you to every one of you who helped. You are ... priceless.

IMPACT PRICING

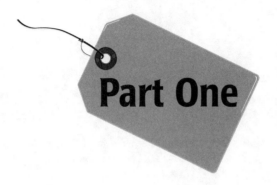

Part One

Pricing Fundamentals:
What You Need to Know

It is a socialist idea that making profits is a vice. I consider the real vice is making losses.

—Winston Churchill

Chapter 1

Vision:
See Where Your Pricing Needs to Go

Throughout the centuries there were men who took first steps, down new roads, armed with nothing but their own vision.

—Ayn Rand

Key Concepts

✔ Align your pricing strategies to help execute your company's vision and overall strategies.

✔ Startups looking to raise money should determine what improves their market capitalization, then price to meet that objective.

✔ Do not use low prices as your overall strategy unless you are willing to dedicate your entire company to lowering costs.

When you select a pricing strategy, what is your objective? The first answer that comes to mind may be to maximize profits. But that's not enough.

For example, when your company develops new products, what's the goal? To maximize profits. But that doesn't tell you what types of products to develop.

IMPACT PRICING

When your company invests in a new marketing campaign what's the goal? To maximize profits. But that doesn't tell you which customer to target or what message to deliver.

Similarly, pricing strategy requires more direction than simply maximizing profits.

Both Ikea and Mercedes want to maximize profits, but they do so using very different pricing strategies. Yet we don't think of Ikea and Mercedes in terms of their pricing strategies, we think of them in terms of their products and positioning. Ikea is a fun, designer, starter furniture store; Mercedes is a luxury automobile manufacturer.

Both companies set their pricing strategies to be consistent with their overall goals, with the vision of who they are.

Strategy Is a Communication Tool

A CEO develops the vision of where the company is heading. He or she then develops several overall strategies on how to achieve that vision. Apple's strategy is to make consumer electronics that are elegant and easy to use. BMW's strategy is to build fantastic cars. Lew Gerstner famously changed IBM's strategy from computer hardware into IT solutions to include both hardware and services.

Your overall strategy is the general description of how you compete in the market. It is your sustainable competitive advantage. Your strategy should be based on how your product or service differs from your competition. The basis for your strategy can be product features, it can be location, it can be marketing, it can be breadth or focus of offering. It can be many things, but it shouldn't be price (with one exception discussed later in this chapter).

Vision and strategies are how a company aligns its people to work toward the same results. If you have employees, you provide them guidance through your vision and your strategies. Vision and strategy start out as a clean expression from

Vision: See Where Your Pricing Needs to Go

the CEO, but each level in a company has to add to them, clarify them, develop their own strategies so the people in that area know what to do. For example, the VP of Engineering, knowing the vision and strategies of the CEO, must create objectives and strategies so the engineers know what's expected of them. These strategies may include what development platforms they'll use or their quality control procedures. You may think of these as important processes. For purposes of this section, think of them as strategies for the department. If the VP has directors or managers, these lower levels may develop objectives and strategies for achieving those goals.

Strategies are the persistent processes or procedures that a manager, director, VP, or CEO uses to help the team deliver on the objectives.

Pricing strategies are no different. Typically a marketing person will be the one to determine the price for a product, but he or she does this under the guidance of the processes and procedures established by the person developing the pricing strategy.

It is critical that the pricing strategy is developed to support the company strategy. For example, if a company's strategy is like Apple's, building a high-end, highly differentiated brand, then aggressive discounting can severely damage the brand and the company. For a company whose strategy is low pricing, like Walmart, then being caught with high prices on even a few products could damage their reputation. These are two extreme examples, but no matter what your vision and strategies are, pricing plays a major role and must be consistent.

Who should develop the pricing strategy in your company? Hopefully you since you're reading this book. In small companies the CEO and/or VP of marketing usually determine the pricing strategies. If this is you, be sure to read the next section on high-tech startup strategies.

IMPACT PRICING

In large corporations, rarely does a clear hierarchy exist for setting pricing strategies. Companies that have explicit pricing groups have them reporting to finance, marketing, or the product lines, sometimes even sales. Regardless of where they report, many people in different functional areas of an organization are extremely interested in, if not involved with, pricing. Because of this, strategic pricing decisions are typically challenging to make. Oftentimes functional areas within a company meet to make these decisions collaboratively, but the competing demands of sales (lower prices) and the product line (higher prices) tend to escalate these decisions to the upper levels of an organization.

The key takeaway from this section is you have to know your company's vision and overall strategies. Only after these are clear should you attempt to create a pricing strategy. The pricing strategy will either help or hinder the company in its actions to fulfill that vision.

Market Cap Pricing

Strategy is how you will achieve your objective. One objective most companies have is to *maximize the market cap of the company*. Market cap is short for market capitalization and means the total value of the company. If an investor wanted to purchase the entire company, the market cap is basically the price.

Public Corporations

In public companies market cap is calculated by taking the number of shares outstanding times the price per share. The executive who wants to increase the value of the company does so by trying to increase the stock price. CEOs and CFOs of most public companies expend significant mental energy determining how to grow their market cap (increase stock price). The CEO does this by setting a corporate strategy and, as discussed in the previous section, each func-

Vision: See Where Your Pricing Needs to Go

tional area below that level sets their own objectives and strategies to execute the strategy set by the CEO.

The CEO of a company I worked with believed that increasing ASP (average selling price) and margins would increase the value of their stock. Consistent with his beliefs, he set the company strategy to increase the profit margin and ASP. This included where to invest R&D resources, which markets to target, and which manufacturing processes to develop. Knowing this vision and strategy, the pricing department was then able to create several pricing strategies to help achieve this. For example they were more aggressive on pricing higher ASP, higher margin business, and less flexible with the lower ASP, lower margin business. In this example the CEO set a strategy with the objective to grow market cap, and the pricing organization created strategies to achieve the corporate strategy.

Regardless of the CEO's strategy to increase stock price, pricing almost always plays an important role.

Entrepreneurial Startups

Maximizing market cap for entrepreneurial startups (who typically are looking to raise the next round of funding) is even more interesting. While the CEO of a public company focuses on the stock price, the CEO of a startup must focus on *how potential future investors will value the company*. Startup companies get "valued" when an investment event happens.

For example, each session on the ABC show *Shark Tank* starts out with the announcer saying something like "This entrepreneur is looking for $50,000 in exchange for 20 percent of her company." By asking for this exchange, she believes her company is worth $250,000. This value is calculated by dividing the investment by the share given up or $50K/20%. If she is lucky, after hearing her pitch, one of the sharks (investors) will offer her something like "I'll give you

IMPACT PRICING

$75K for 50 percent of your company." The shark is saying, "Your company is only worth $150,000 to me."

The math here isn't important. What's important is that the entrepreneur must build the company, including products, services, and pricing, to be attractive to potential investors. She wants the sharks to believe her company is worth a lot.

> • In startups, the pricing decision is vital to the company's market cap.

#impactpricing

The startup executive must consciously determine what maximizes the value of the company. In the late 1990s, investors famously invested based on the number of "eyeballs" at an Internet site. During those times Internet companies were focused almost exclusively on how many visitors they could attract to their site and how long each visitor would stay. Price was free or as close to it as possible. The eyeballs generated market cap.

In today's world, investors look more at how many customers a company has served and at what price. They estimate future sales and profit margins to guess at the future profitability and therefore future value of the company.

Public companies tend to be large, and individual pricing decisions have little effect on the stock value. In startup companies, the pricing decision is vital to the company's market cap. Initial pricing decisions are almost always made by the CEO and/or VP of marketing.

Startups often break new ground, putting a first price on a new product in a new market without historic examples to follow. There may be very few market indicators on how to set the price. An executive must create the pricing strategy while setting these first prices. This is where market cap pricing is critical.

As a startup executive, you know that if you want to

Vision: See Where Your Pricing Needs to Go

maximize your number of customers you need prices to be very low or even free. The faster your ramp rate of new customers, the more likely the investors will accept your predictions of huge future sales.

However, investors also look closely at your profit margin to see how much money you can make when your idea takes off. The good news is they may look at projected profit margin using your projected future costs rather than your current costs. If you have a realistic belief that your costs will decrease significantly and rapidly, you may want to "forward price" your products, which means pricing as though you already have those lower costs. In some circumstances you may set your prices below your current costs. You can justify the losses as part of your product launch expenses. Of course, you must have pockets deep enough to cover these losses. This strategy allows you to capture customers more quickly.

Your job, when determining the pricing strategy for your startup company, is to charge a price low enough to capture enough customers to prove to potential investors the idea is a great one. And, at the same time, you need to keep prices high enough that your investors see the idea is or will be profitable. As an executive at a startup, you must understand what maximizes your market capitalization before making this critical decision. What do your investors want to see?

Market cap pricing is your reminder that, as an executive of a startup, your pricing decisions have a dramatic impact on the amount investors will value your company. Price wisely.

Small Businesses

If you're an owner of a small business you're probably not worried about market cap. Instead, you're looking to earn a steadily growing income from your business. Large corporations and high-tech startups worry about profitability among other things because it influences their market cap. Your

IMPACT PRICING

key objective is profitability for its own sake. Profitability is how you put food on your table.

Most of the pricing strategies presented in this book can work well for you. Pricing plays a major role in profitability.

Nonfinancial Objectives

> Each Walmart store should reflect the values of its customers and support the vision they hold for their community.
> —Sam Walton

#impactpricing

As described above, CEOs typically translate their unstated objective of maximizing shareholder value into more actionable objectives, like increase profitability (short term and long term), grow revenue, raise average selling price, increase market share, grow gross margin, and many more. Each of these is a financial objective that pricing can directly and efficiently impact. A good pricing organization will adjust the pricing strategies to help achieve all of them.

> Pricing strategy follows the corporate strategy. Set your corporate strategy first.

#impactpricing

However, some companies don't attempt to maximize market capitalization. These companies have multiple objectives that include both financial and nonfinancial goals. For example, many companies manage to a socially conscious objective. Ben and Jerry's quickly jumps to mind with their explicit policies on altruistic giving. Chick-Fil-A is a privately held company that is as concerned with its community service as it is with its profits. How do you set prices in an environment like that? Are you trying to make money so you can give it away? Are you trying to keep prices low out of a social conscience? The answer on how to set prices is ... it depends on the corporate strategy. The corporate strategy must be set

Vision: See Where Your Pricing Needs to Go

first and should be detailed enough to inform the pricing team on how to set consistent pricing strategies. Ben and Jerry's ice cream has premium pricing, but they give away a percentage of their profits. Chick-Fil-A intentionally keeps prices lower than they need to as a service to their customers and community.

Price is first and foremost a tool that is best used to achieve financial objectives, but if socially conscious objectives are clearly defined, pricing can play a major role in contributing to them as well. The big takeaway is: Pricing strategy follows the corporate strategy. Set your corporate strategy first.

Low Price as a Corporate Strategy: Don't Do It!

> The bitterness of poor quality is remembered long after the sweetness of low price has faded from memory.
> —Aldo Gucci

#impactpricing

Pricing is not a corporate strategy.

Pricing is not a sustainable competitive advantage. Prices can change almost instantly. Your competitor can change prices just as quickly as you can. What if you find that optimal price, that psychologically perfect price that magically makes all customers want to buy from you? Your competitors will copy it—immediately. Any competitive advantage you may gain with pricing is not sustainable. With one exception ...

The one time that pricing can be a corporate strategy is when the company is positioned as the low price leader. That's Walmart. If you adopt low price as your strategy, then your business must be continually focused on lowering and controlling costs—like Walmart. You are attracting the price buyers, the customers who are not loyal, but are looking for the lowest price. Once a competitor figures out how to sell a

IMPACT PRICING

similar product for less, they will charge lower prices, and you will struggle. If another company figures out how to sell products for less than Walmart, Walmart will be in trouble. Knowing this, Walmart maintains a laser-sharp focus on keeping costs down. If you make low price your strategy, you have to be like Walmart, continuously lowering your costs so your competitors don't catch up.

You may be thinking about a different price-based strategy. "My product is as good as a Lexus, but less expensive. I'm going to make that my strategy." Don't do it. You may be able to have that product positioning for a short while, but it's not sustainable. The market will morph, and your position may or may not exist in a few years. You have competitors on both sides of you, above and below, either of which may be able to steal your position, because your position is just price. A better strategy would be to position your company relative to a Toyota, differentiate your products, then price to the market.

Let's look again at Walmart in competition with other discount retail stores. Kmart is having a difficult time competing with Walmart. Same-store sales continue to decline even as they come out of the 2010 recession. On the other hand, Target's same-store sales figures are growing rapidly. What's the difference? Although there are many factors, one is that Target has a unique positioning. It is described as "trendy," "cool," "a hip discounter." Kmart may have the Martha Stewart brand, but the company as a whole doesn't own a position. There doesn't seem to be any real differentiation between Kmart and Walmart (other than price, which Walmart wins).

> Anybody can cut prices, but it takes brains to make a better article.
> —Philip Armour

#impactpricing

Vision: See Where Your Pricing Needs to Go

Target's success isn't because they are a discount retailer. They would not be able to beat Walmart in a low price battle. Target's success is because they are the "hip discounter." They own a unique positioning. There is only room for one company with lowest prices, and that company is Walmart, at least for now.

The strategy of low-cost leader is a rough-and-tumble position. Everything is done without frills. Once you get too comfortable, someone else hungrier than you will do it with less and steal your position. This is not a fun position to defend. Kmart used to be the low price leader. Then Walmart created better systems, had lower cost processes, and because of its better cost structure was able to displace Kmart as the low price leader. Now Kmart is floundering. What will happen to Walmart when it gets complacent, or someone else comes up with lower-cost solutions?

Even if you don't use the low-cost strategy, you must still focus some of your energy and resources on costs. Target, Kmart, and every company in a competitive situation still win and lose customers based on their prices, and if they want to have competitive prices, they must maintain relatively low costs. Price is a factor in every customer's decision, and if one company's costs are much higher than another's, then they run the risk of losing on price. Even though low-price leader is not your strategy, you still must control your costs.

> Customers today want the very most and the very best for the very least amount of money, and on the best terms. Only the individuals and companies that provide absolutely excellent products and services at absolutely excellent prices will survive.
>
> —Brian Tracy

#impactpricing

IMPACT PRICING

Summary

This chapter described how pricing strategy and corporate strategy are tightly related. Before creating an effective pricing strategy, the company must have a clear vision of the desired future and a set of corporate strategies on how to reach that vision. Pricing strategy contributes to these corporate strategies.

Corporate strategies are frequently financial in nature, which lead to clear pricing strategies. However, some companies have nonfinancial strategies. Pricing can often contribute to these nonfinancial strategies, as well. The key is explicitly knowing the company strategies so the pricing team (person) can create appropriate pricing strategies.

Pricing has a large impact on market capitalization or the overall value of the company. In a large corporation, the CEO sets a corporate strategy he or she believes will increase the stock price, and pricing strategies follow directly from that. In fast-growing startups though, the CEO must determine what will most impress potential investors, with the objective being to cause these investor to value the company highly. Pricing is absolutely critical at this stage in the startup.

The final section emphasized that you should think very carefully before deciding to compete on price. Making low price your strategy attracts the next company who thinks it can do what you do just a little cheaper. This commits you to always be focused on taking out costs.

As you finish this first chapter, I hope you now realize that before you can select the right pricing strategies, you must clearly know the overall company strategies. Do you?

Vision: See Where Your Pricing Needs to Go

Summary Questions

✔ What is your overall strategy? Write it down.

✔ Is your overall strategy based on price or differentiation?

✔ What measurable outcomes will increase your market capitalization?

✔ What nonfinancial objectives does your company have? How can pricing help?

Actions: What are you going to do?

Chapter 2

Pricing Strategies:
A First Glance

There is nothing in the world that some man cannot make a little worse and sell a little cheaper, and he who considers price only is that man's lawful prey.

—John Ruskin

Key Concepts

✔ Value-based pricing is the fundamental pricing strategy.

✔ Know when to use neutral, penetration, and skim pricing.

✔ Use penetration pricing to grow the market, not market share alone.

✔ Pricing strategy depends on the market type, negotiated or TIOLI.

Price may not be the basis of your corporate strategy, but you *must* have a pricing strategy to implement your corporate strategy. Remember that pricing strategies are big-picture decisions that provide guidance to the people within your organization who actually set prices. They are your pricing processes and policies.

IMPACT PRICING

As you read through this book, especially Parts Two and Three, you will learn many pricing strategies. This chapter touches on three strategic decisions to understand and think about early in this process.

Neutral, Penetration, and Skimming

When you ask a marketer "What are some pricing strategies?", you will likely get the answer that there are three pricing strategies: *neutral*, *penetration*, and *skimming*. Do a Google search on "pricing strategy," and you'll find the same answer over and over: neutral, penetration, and skimming. These certainly are pricing strategies, but they are not the only ones. A better way to look at this is that these are pricing strategies to define the *general level* of prices. As you will read throughout this book, companies make many strategic pricing decisions. But while we're on the topic, let's review neutral, penetration, and skimming.

Neutral pricing, the most common pricing strategy, means that you price so that your customers are relatively indifferent between your product and your competitor's product after all features and benefits, including price, are taken into account. Of course not all customers will be indifferent. Some will like your offering better, others will like your competitor's better. From this perspective, think of neutral pricing as maintaining the status quo. You aren't trying to gain or lose market share. Most pricing in relatively stable markets would be considered neutral. As you walk through a grocery store, the prices you see are neutral. Although you may use a combination of neutral, penetration, and skimming prices, you will most often use neutral.

Penetration pricing means pricing more aggressively than neutral. It can be used to gain market share relative to your competition—but be careful. This can and does start price wars. (See the section on price wars in Chapter 17.) No company wants to lose market share, and if you lower your price

Pricing Strategies: A First Glance

in an effort to gain market share, your competitors are likely to lower their prices just to keep their share.

A more appropriate and common use of penetration pricing is to speed up the growth of a newly forming market. Low pricing is often justified to quickly grow a new market and to gain the largest share as the market grows. This strategy works best when you are the first entrant, or one of the first entrants, into a market. Penetration pricing in this situation may also deter other companies from competing when they recognize there are not huge profits to be gained.

Forward pricing is another term similar to penetration pricing, but with a focus on future costs. If you're building a product and it costs $1 to make, you probably don't want to sell it for less than $1. However, if you know that once you sell a million units, your costs will go down to $0.30, you may be willing to sell at a price lower than your current costs knowing that your costs will be lower in the future. The forward part of the name indicates you're looking forward in time to estimate what your costs will be and using that cost as your basis for pricing.

Skimming is the opposite of penetration pricing. Companies skim in an effort to segment the market, to get the customers who are willing to pay more to do so. The two common implementations of skimming are at new product launch and at the end of a product's life.

When companies skim during new product launch, they are selling to customers with a high willingness to pay. Once this market is depleted (or at least slows down), then the company lowers the price to sell to the next tier of customers. A recent, famous example of this was the initial release of the Apple iPhone. Apple released the iPhone on September 5, 2007, for $599. Apple fans rushed out to purchase the iPhone. Two months later Apple lowered the price to $399 to capture even more customers. The earliest adopters paid

IMPACT PRICING

$200 more for the privilege of being first. In this case, though, Apple got a black eye. The huge price decrease was too much too soon according to the early adopters. Remember, these early adopters were big fans and Apple risked losing significant customer goodwill from these, their best customers. Apple eventually gave each of the early adopters a $100 store credit.

There are also cases where a company should be able to skim, but doesn't. In 1998, Volkswagen re-released its redesigned once-popular Beetle. Demand far exceeded supply, and VW couldn't make them quickly enough. Although you had to be on a waiting list to get a new Beetle, you could purchase a used one for thousands of dollars over the MSRP. Shouldn't VW have charged more and captured those thousands of dollars for itself? Possibly, but VW decided that it was best not to skim. This gave VW additional goodwill and, more importantly, free media attention and a feeling of scarcity, which only heightened consumer desire.

Skimming as a market entry strategy only works when you have a monopolistic position (both the iPhone and the Beetle were unique). The lesson from Apple's case is to bring your price down slowly. The news articles at the time didn't berate Apple for lowering the price, they berated it for lowering the price too soon.

The other common use of skimming is at a product's end of life. Sometimes firms would like to discontinue a product but have too many customers who have a continuing need for it. In this situation the company may gradually increase prices over market value to gain more revenue from these customers. The firm is trading off being able to compete for new business for additional revenue on existing business. One big caution is that customers, especially loyal customers like these, don't like to have their prices raised. You must have a good explanation and possibly an alternative offering.

Pricing Strategies: A First Glance

It should be apparent that these three strategies follow specific corporate objectives. If a corporate objective is to raise ASP (average selling price), then skimming may be appropriate. If a corporate objective is to win market share, then penetration pricing is needed. If the corporate strategy is to generate and capture value, then neutral pricing would be appropriate.

A company doesn't just choose one of these strategies and is done. Each of these three strategies can be used by the same company, depending on the customer or the product. Recall that penetration and skimming were best applied to new products in new markets. As market conditions change, so should your pricing strategy. That leads us to look at several other pricing strategies.

Value-Based Pricing

Value-based pricing is the most important concept in this book. The idea seems simple. How much is your customer willing to pay? Set the price at or just below that point.

However, the implementation and usage of value-based pricing is much more complex. Chapters 3 and 4 are devoted to understanding the fundamentals of value-based pricing. Every strategy presented in Parts Two and Three assume you use value-based pricing.

Throughout business history, firms traditionally used the cost-plus method of determining prices. They determined how much their product cost to make and then added whatever margin they thought they deserved. Hence, the term cost-plus. Cost-plus pricing has some advantages: it's simple, you don't have to understand your customers, and it's easy for you and your competitors to get in sync. However,

> Charge what the customers are willing to pay.

#impactpricing

cost-plus is not optimal pricing.

You have to make a strategic pricing decision. Are you going to use cost-plus pricing or value-based pricing (or some other method)? If you want to increase profits, you will commit to using value-based pricing. As you learn more about value-based pricing, you'll learn that it's impossible to implement perfectly. After all, our customers never tell us exactly how much they're willing to pay. However, value-based pricing is accepted by pricing professionals and consultants as the optimal pricing strategy.

This isn't a trivial, lightly adopted concept. Nor is it easy for many people to accept. It's a commitment. It requires constant communication and vigilant observation of pricing behaviors. I have worked with many people, including pricing professionals, who told me they use value-based pricing, but when they needed to make certain decisions they fell back on cost-plus pricing methods. It's hard to let go of traditional ways of thinking.

Most large corporations have committed to value-based pricing and have implemented it with some degree of success. Unfortunately, most smaller companies don't know what it is. This is an opportunity for small and medium-sized businesses to catch up.

The concept is simple: *Charge what the customers are willing to pay*. The implementation and internalization are not as easy.

> If you don't get what you want, it's a sign either that you did not seriously want it, or that you tried to bargain over the price.
>
> —Rudyard Kipling

#impactpricing

Negotiated vs. TIOLI Pricing

The third strategy for this chapter is how you'll deliver your

Pricing Strategies: A First Glance

prices. Will you negotiate each deal, or will you set a price and let customers take it or leave it (TIOLI)? The right answer to this question will be obvious for your market and, in most cases, is closely correlated with whether you are in a B2B or B2C market.

In B2C markets, shoppers have very little power. When a consumer shops for a book from Amazon.com, his only choice is to purchase or not purchase. This is called a TIOLI market. Almost every consumer market uses TIOLI pricing, where the customers' only power is their ability to choose whether or not to purchase. Books, groceries, gasoline, clothing, airline tickets, and haircuts are all examples of product categories where the price is given and the consumer then makes a purchase decision. The two consumer purchases that are typically not TIOLI are homes and cars. In both cases the buyer usually negotiates a final price with the seller.

B2B customers frequently have more power than consumers. When Dell buys processors from Intel, Dell is buying so many millions of units that they have a lot of power. Dell has so much power that the two firms regularly negotiate their prices. Intel does not have the power (or desire) to just set a price and let Dell take it or leave it. If Dell leaves it, Intel would be out millions of dollars. B2B markets frequently have negotiated prices, especially when the size of the customer's purchase is very large. However, B2B markets also maintain TIOLI prices, typically through distribution, where they sell to smaller customers. A small computer motherboard manufacturer would not be allowed to negotiate pricing directly with Intel. Instead it would buy processors from distributors like Digi-Key or Arrow Electronics.

Negotiated vs. TIOLI pricing isn't really a decision you get to make. The market makes it for you. Yet this is a concept you want to understand so you know how to apply the strategies presented in the remainder of the book. Many of the pricing strategies we look at going forward apply equally to negotiated and TIOLI markets. However, when a strategy only applies to one of these, it will be pointed out.

Summary

The traditional answer to "what are pricing strategies?" is neutral, skim, and penetration. Neutral is pricing to keep the status quo. Penetration pricing is used to grow the market quickly, but should probably not be used to grow market share if the market isn't growing. Skimming is used either when releasing a monopolistic product or at the end of a product's life.

Neutral, penetration, and skim pricing are important strategies, but value-based pricing impacts your profitability more than any other. The idea is easy: Charge what customers are willing to pay. You'll want to adopt this concept. Knowing, believing, and internalizing value-based pricing enables you to understand and adopt many more pricing strategies to come. But don't worry if you haven't completely absorbed it yet. Chapters 3 and 4 walk you through the concepts and the process.

Finally, although you don't have control over it, you should know what type of market you are in—negotiated or TIOLI. This will be relevant as you read the remainder of this

Pricing Strategies: A First Glance

book and come up with new pricing strategies on your own.

Summary Questions

- ✔ What new products do you have coming out where penetration pricing would be optimal?
- ✔ What new products do you have coming out where skimming would be optimal?
- ✔ What products are at the end of life where skimming may be optimal?
- ✔ Do you currently use value-based pricing? If not, are you ready to commit?
- ✔ What percent of your revenue comes from TIOLI business?

Actions: What are you going to do?

Chapter 3

Value: What Is Your Product Worth?

Old boys have their playthings as well as young ones, the difference is only in the price.

—Benjamin Franklin

Key Concepts

- ✔ Product development creates real value. Customers buy perceived value.
- ✔ Marketers create perceived value. Perceived value is most easily derived from real value.
- ✔ Three different types of value: choice value, value in use, and overall value.
- ✔ Customers make two buying decisions. Will I? and Which one? Price has a much bigger effect on "Which one?"
- ✔ Customers trade off differences in attributes for differences in prices.

The concept of value-based pricing is to "charge what the customer is willing to pay." How much do they value your product? The hardest part of value-based pricing is determining (well, estimating) what your customers are willing to pay. The easiest way to think about your value to your customers is to put yourself in their shoes. This chapter provides a model—an intuitive description—of how your customers think about value. In the next chapter we use this model to put a price on one of your products.

Customers Buy Perceived Value

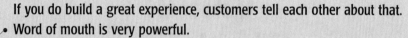

> If you do build a great experience, customers tell each other about that. Word of mouth is very powerful.
>
> —Jeff Bezos
>
> #impactpricing

The value of a product or service is measured by how much your customers are willing to pay for it. The price you decide to charge should be your best estimate of your customers' willingness to pay. In its simplest form, your potential customers compare your product with your competitor's product and your price with your competitor's price. If they decide to buy a product in this category, they will buy the one that they think is the best deal for them. (As always, the term *product* means products, services, and all of the pieces of the offering like warranty, support, delivery, etc.).

So how much is your customer willing to pay for your product? It depends on how much your competitor charges and, most important, how your product differs from your competitor's in its ability to solve a customer problem or fill a customer need.

If your product is better than your competitor's, you can charge the price your competitor charges *plus* the amount your customers value your product over the competition's. If your competitor's product is better than yours, then you must charge less than your competitor to win some of the business.

You're probably saying, "This is just common sense." And it is. But the important lesson is that the amount your cus-

Value: What Is Your Product Worth?

tomers are willing to pay is not based on your cost. The amount they're willing to pay is based on your competitor's price and the value of roduct differences. This is the essence of *value-based pricing*.

You create real value by improving your products and services relative to your competition. You create real value when you add a new benefit, when you improve quality, when customer service smiles more often, when you lengthen your warranty.

However, customers don't buy real value, they buy perceived value. What do they think about your product? You may have the best product attribute in the world, but if the customers don't know about it or don't believe your claim or think it's worth the extra cost, they won't pay you a premium for it. Product development creates real value. Marketing and sales create perceived value. The best and easiest marketing plans simply make sure prospects know your real value. In other words, create perceived value by building real value and then communicate honestly about it.

> Customers don't buy real value, they buy perceived value.

#impactpricing

Apple is excellent at creating perceived value. Compare a Mac to a PC. PCs have more hardware features because they are based on an open platform. PCs have more software available, partly because Microsoft focuses on PCs, but mostly because it is an open platform with a very large user base so software developers have a larger market for their offerings. So if PCs have more hardware and software features, why are Macs so much more expensive for similar products? Apple has created a brand image of simplicity and "cool." Some people have a strong belief that Macs are easier to use, and I've never met a Mac user who wasn't proud to tell me he or she used a Mac. Many people perceive Macs to have much more value than PCs so are willing to pay the premium. Apple has done a superb job of creating perceived value. Nothing derogatory is implied by this statement. Apple builds great products, but just as important, the company has great marketing. Apple's marketing does a phenomenal job of converting real value into perceived value.

Which platform is really better, Mac or PC? By how much? There is no objective answer to those questions. What matters in this example though, is that *the facts are less important than the perceptions of the buyers.* Consumers buy perceived value. Apple has created enough perceived value in many peoples' minds to be able to charge a nice premium.

Price is the marketing lever that turns perceived value into revenue. Think of it like a value scorecard. The more value you create and communicate, the higher the score. As an executive, you should direct the majority of your company resources toward creating real and perceived value for your customers. However, effective pricing does require resources, investment in people, processes, and systems, especially for large corporations. Once the company creates all this value, be sure to capture as much of it as possible.

One critically important byproduct of studying pricing is it points out areas where you can create more value. As you compare your products with your competition, you will look for differentiation because that's where the value is. Your next products will probably have even more differentiation. You will listen to your customers and whether they value your the differentiations you've built into your offerings. If they don't, you'll put more resources into marketing to elevate your customers' perceptions. Pricing does a wonderful job at clarifying other areas in the company that could be improved.

Your engineering and product development teams create real value. Your marketing and sales organizations create

Value: What Is Your Product Worth?

perceived value. Your pricing team (person) measures the amount of perceived value created and puts a number on it.

Choice Value, Value in Use, and Deal Value

Value is a common word, but it has three different meanings in the world of pricing. Whenever we hear that word used by a customer, a colleague, or a consultant, we need to know what this individual means. The three meanings (or types) of value are *choice* value, value *in use*, and *overall* value. When we use the phrase *value-based pricing*, we are usually talking about choice value.

Choice Value

Choice value is the amount of value a customer perceives from our product relative to our competitor's product when deciding which one to purchase.

If a prospect is deciding between a Ford Taurus and a Toyota Camry, and the Ford Taurus costs $30,000, then how much would she be willing to pay for the Camry? In other words, how much does she *value* the Camry relative to the Taurus?

Choice value is how much a customer is willing to pay for a product, knowing the price of her next best alternative. This is the meaning implied in the phrase v*alue-based pricing*. Almost all of our pricing decisions are made trying to understand how our customers value our product vis-à-vis the competition, so this is the most common meaning for pricers. Throughout this chapter and the remainder of this book, there are several examples of choice value decisions. When the word *value* is used without a modifier, the implied meaning is choice value.

Value in Use

Value in use is the amount of value a person receives from using a product. How much does someone value air? Air is

IMPACT PRICING

essential to breathing, and breathing is essential to life. The value (in use) of air is practically infinite. Most people would likely pay everything they have for air if they had to. As you can see from this example, even though air is free it has an extremely high value (in use) to us.

> When the well is dry, we will know the worth of water.
> —Benjamin Franklin

#impactpricing

How much does a person value owning a car to drive to work? She could walk. She could ride a bike. She could take a bus or other public transportation. She may be willing to pay up to $500 per month to have her own car to drive. Thus, her value in use would be that $500 every month.

Think of value in use as the value used while budgeting. Most people have limited income and need to allocate it to many dissimilar expenses: mortgage, car, food, education, clothes, entertainment, and more. How do they decide how much each of these is worth to them? If they decide they can only afford a $500-per-month car payment, then that limits their choice of cars.

Value in use is relevant to pricers in that it determines the number of potential customers, but choice value is far more important when making pricing decisions. The one time that value in use is more important than choice value is for brand-new products with no direct competition. For example, when Apple released the new iPad, there were no real competitors in this category. Sure there were a few tablet PCs available, but Apple created a new market. They had to determine the value in use of an iPad to their customers when setting their price. Customers were not choosing between the iPad and the Tablet PC, they were deciding whether to buy an iPad or nothing and saving that money for another purpose.

Value: What Is Your Product Worth?

Overall Value

Choice value and value in use are both about value exclusive of price. In fact, the implied measure for value in those two definitions was price. Notice that in both descriptions, the phrase "willing to pay" was used as a measure of value.

Overall value includes price. It means the combined value of the product and price. Overall value drives the answer to the question "Did you get a good deal?"

For example, after a buyer purchased a new Taurus, she might say to her neighbor, "This was a great value." Similarly, she might say that she didn't buy the Camry because it wasn't a good value. A Camry at $20,000 might be a great value, but a Camry at $35,000 might not be.

Overall value relates to what someone expected to pay for the product. What they expect to pay is also called their *reference price*. So a great value is when the price is much lower than their reference price. You'll read more about reference prices in a later chapter.

Will I? Which One?

Will I? Which one? These are two questions your customers ask themselves and answer every time they deliberate about a purchase. Will I buy a product (or service) in this category? If so, which one will I buy? If someone is in the market to buy a new car (Will I?—Yes), then she is probably looking at her options (Which one?). If she is not in the market for a new car (Will I?—No), then she probably isn't shopping around. Before a shopper chooses which bag of chips to buy (Which one?), she first must decide that she wants a bag of chips (Will I?—Yes).

Let's explore these two buying decisions your customers make.

IMPACT PRICING

Will I?

Before making a purchase, customers must decide to purchase a product in your product category. In other words, they have to choose to allocate money from their limited income or budget to your industry. Recall the meaning of value in use from above. If they have a high value in use relative to the general prices in your product category, then the customer will consider purchasing something from you or your competitor.

Pricing is relatively powerless at convincing someone to purchase a product in a specific category. Pricing is much more powerful when influencing consumer choice within a category (the "Which one?" decision). Buyers typically require very large price changes to influence a change to their budget, but relatively small price changes to influence their product choice behavior.

However, there are three circumstances where pricing influences the "Will I?" decision that leads directly to purchase without a "Which one?" decision. First, if you have a monopoly. When Pacific Gas and Electric raises my electricity prices, I think about how to use less electricity. This is an example of me choosing to purchase less in the product category.

Second, in brand-new product categories, pricing plays a major role in potential customers' choosing to purchase or not. We previously discussed the iPad in this context. Now let's look at a hypothetical example. If a pharmaceutical company invented a drug that would make us lose weight (one that actually worked), how would they price this? There isn't really any competition, so price wouldn't be based on choice value. Instead, they would estimate how many people value (in use) the pill at different prices and set their prices based on whether people will buy in the category. In this case, think of brand-new product categories as short-term monopolies where the pioneer has a monopoly until competition enters the market.

Value: What Is Your Product Worth?

Is the new product like an aspirin or a vitamin? This is an interesting analogy to help understand how much value potential customers place on a new product. Customers pay a lot for aspirin-like solutions, ones that solve a real problem or somehow ease our pain. Customers tend to undervalue vitamin-like solutions, ones that are good for us, but don't solve an immediate problem. The weight loss pill discussed above would certainly be an aspirin-like product, solving the pain of millions of people who don't wish to be overweight.

Third, price can affect the "Will I?" decision when there are large decreases in the lowest price in a market. In many markets, especially relatively new ones, there are a lot of potential customers who have not yet chosen to purchase a product in the category because even the lowest-priced item is too expensive relative to their income. Even today, many Chinese do not own television sets. However, as the price of TVs comes down dramatically, which has happened recently, more people purchase them. This is a highly elastic market exhibiting much higher sales as a result of price reductions.

Although we have identified three instances where pricing influences purchases directly through the "Will I?" decision, this is the exception, not the rule. There are other examples as well, like pricing for impulse purchases, where the consumer does not compare alternatives. Even in these situations where "Will I?" decisions lead directly to purchases, price does not play that large of a role. It takes large price changes to get someone to change their "Will I?" behavior while much smaller price changes can influence the "Which one?" decision.

Which One?

Customers make choices. With a few exceptions, they choose between relatively similar offerings every time they make a purchase. They choose which car to buy, which computer to purchase, which laundromat to frequent, which airline to fly,

IMPACT PRICING

which realtor to use, and which restaurants to visit. B2B buyers are even more deliberate when choosing their suppliers.

> There is only one boss. The customer. And he can fire everybody in the company from the chairman on down, simply by spending his money somewhere else.
>
> —Sam Walton

#impactpricing

Potential customers trade off perceived attributes with price. Because the features of the alternatives are often similar, small differences in price can swing a purchase decision. In the world of pricing, this is where the leverage is. Not only is the "Which one?" decision most commonly the last decision the customer makes, it is also the decision where price has the biggest influence. As you might guess almost all of the remainder of this book focuses on pricing for the "Which one?" decision.

We need our product development team to create real value by differentiating our products from those of our competitors. We need our marketing team to translate this difference into significant perceived value to influence the "Which one?" decision. And then we want to use this differentiation, this added value, to price this offering as high as we can, as long as the customer chooses our product over our competitors' products.

"Will I?" "Which one?" is a simple concept, but I use it a lot when coaching small businesses to determine what pricing model to use. Every time you approach a pricing problem you need to know which one of these is the final decision. If the customer buys your product after answering only the "Will I?" decision, then you need to use a different pricing model than if the customer goes on to ask and answer the "Which one?" decision.

Customers make choices all day long. They answer "Which one?" with their purchase decisions. As pricers we

Value: What Is Your Product Worth?

focus most on influencing this "Which one?" decision. The next section puts a decision framework around how our customers choose "which one." We will then use this decision framework to help us determine optimal prices.

Elasticity

Price elasticity is a common term frequently used incorrectly (at least according to economists, if that matters). The confusion with its use is directly related to the "Will I?" and "Which one?" questions. Price elasticity means when an industry lowers price by some percentage, sales increase by some percentage. Notice the use of the word "industry." This industry perspective of elasticity means that as industry prices come down, more and more people answer yes to the "Will I?" question. Compare the percentage increase in units sold with the percentage decrease in price, and you have elasticity. The example above about televisions in China was a highly elastic market where unit sales increased quickly as industry prices decreased.

However, many people incorrectly use elasticity referring to similar effects that happen at the company level. When a company lowers prices a little and generates a large increase in unit sales, that's a good result for the company. It just doesn't mean elasticity. In this scenario, customers are likely choosing the company's product over the competitive alternative they would have purchased. Industry sales don't increase but company sales do. This is because the price changes are affecting the customer's decision when answering the "Which one?" question.

Because the phrase *price elasticity* is so often misused and confused, I rarely use it in conversations and will not use it again in this text. The caution to you is when you hear someone say "price elasticity," you need to understand the intended meaning. It may mean that as industry prices go down, the market size increases. It may mean that as your company decreases prices, sales increase. The first meaning implies influencing the "Will I?" decision. The latter implies influencing "Which one?" There is a big difference in meanings here and appropriate actions.

Your Customer's Brain—Value-Based Buying

Value-based *pricing* is the most highly recommended pricing technique by consultants and academics. The concept is setting a price to capture the majority of what your customers are willing to pay. Before studying value-based pricing, let's look at value-based *buying*, how your customers make their decisions when they deliberate about which product to purchase.

> With businesses, you go to the same places because you like the service, you like the people, and they take care of you. They greet you with a smile. That's how people want to be treated, with respect. That's what I tell my employees. Customer service is very important.
> —Earvin "Magic" Johnson

#impactpricing

Imagine Sally is at the grocery and she wants to buy a can of green beans. Two cans catch her eye, Safeway Select is a store brand, and Del Monte is a national brand. Safeway Select costs $1.49, and Del Monte costs $1.69. How does she choose? She asks herself, is the Del Monte can worth 20 cents more?

Is it worth it? To answer this, she thinks of everything that's different between the two cans. She may have had better experiences with the Del Monte brand. One may have less salt. One may be cut differently. One may have a more attractive label. It's completely up to her as to what she thinks is important. After she has determined the important differences, she places a value on these differences and then decides if the Del Monte brand is worth 20 cents more than Safeway Select.

Value: What Is Your Product Worth?

Of course she didn't actually do this analysis or this math, but that is a reasonable representation of how her mind makes the decision. What's going on, what question she's answering probably somewhat unconsciously is "If I buy the Del Monte brand, how can I rationalize paying 20 cents more?"

> I have come to a resolution myself as I hope every good citizen will, never again to purchase any article of foreign manufacture which can be had of American make be the difference of price what it may.
> —Thomas Jefferson

#impactpricing

There is no right or wrong answer here. People have different perceptions of the attributes, and they place different values on those attributes. Some people will prefer Del Monte, and others will prefer Safeway Select. What's important is individuals make choices based on the difference in prices, the perceived differences in attributes, and the amount they value the differences in the attributes. The most you can charge any customer and still win the business is whatever your competitor is charging plus (or minus) the amount that customer values your advantages (or disadvantages).

Notice in our example that we assumed Sally wanted to buy a can of beans, meaning she had already answered yes to "Will I?" The remainder of the example was about how she makes her "Which one?" decision. As you can see, price can strongly impact the "Which one?" choice.

Summary

Before tackling value-based pricing in the next chapter, we need to understand what is meant by value. *Value* is an ambiguous word that we defined in several ways: choice value, value in use, and overall value.

Value in choice is how one product compares to another without considering price. Value in use is how a product compares to all other uses of money. And overall value is the value of the deal after taking price into account.

Another way to think about value is real vs. perceived. Product development teams build real value into the product by adding true product features. Marketing then creates perceived value by communicating the important and differentiated attributes to the customers.

Customers make a "Will I?" decision based on value in use, and then a "Which one?" decision based on value in choice. Pricing has the most effect on the "Which one?" decision. "Which one?" is also the foundation of value-based buying and pricing.

We then apply these concepts stepping through a customer's decision process, which we called value-based buying. Customers make their "Which one?" decision by comparing the perceived differences in attributes of their two best alternatives and weighing the value of these differences against the difference in prices. The customer makes this "Which one" decision by selecting the option with the most value in choice.

Summary Questions

- ✔ Can you identify features of your products that your customers do not perceive as different? Should marketing be communicating about them more?
- ✔ Do you have any new products where you have no competition, where your customers don't have to answer "Which one?"
- ✔ Think through the last (or next) several purchases you made. While deciding "Which one?," how closely did your behaviors follow the value-based buying model?

Actions: What are you going to do?

Chapter 4

Value-Based Pricing:
Mandatory to Maximize Profits

People want economy and they will pay any price to get it."

—Lee Iacocca

Key Concepts

✔ Value-based pricing is the underlying pricing strategy that captures the *most* customer value and turns it into revenue.

✔ Differentiation creates value.

✔ The five steps in value-based pricing change the way you think about pricing.

The previous chapter described how potential customers may make choices between two alternatives. The Del Monte beans are more expensive than the Safeway Select beans, but are they worth more? What is the value of the differences?

Value-based pricing uses that model to determine the price that a potential customer will pay for your product. The process of value-based pricing looks like a formula, which it is. But value-based pricing is much more valuable to you as a framework for thinking about how to set your prices. Every time you think about price, you should be thinking about how your customers make their purchase decisions. When you think about your customers' decisions, you will think about value-based pricing. Internalize this concept and constantly return to it in your pricing conversations with coworkers.

Value Accounting

How much is your product worth? What is the most a customer would pay for it?

You can never know the exact answer to these questions, but when you use the value accounting framework to think about them, you'll make better pricing decisions. Value accounting helps you determine your customer's willingness to pay for your product when making the choice between your offereing and that of one of your competitors.

Let's assume that if your price is too high, then that customer will buy from your competitor. Now, what price could you charge to get him to change his mind and buy from you? Start by finding out how much your competitor is charging. You already know that this customer was willing to pay that amount for your competitor's set of features and benefits.

Now, how is your product better? Estimate how much more your customer would be willing to pay for each of these differentiated benefits. How is your product worse? Estimate how much less your customer would be willing to pay for each of these differentiations. Take the price your competitor charges, add the dollar value of your advantages, and subtract the dollar value of your disadvantages. That is how much your customer is willing to pay.

Let's return to the green bean example from the previous chapter. Imagine that we are Del Monte. Safeway Select

Value-Based Pricing: Mandatory to Maximize Profits

priced its beans at $1.49. We determine that Sally likes our brand name and prefers the amount of salt we use. She values those two features by $0.20. But she likes Safeway Select because she likes helping out her local store. She values that attribute at $0.10. Value accounting shows her willingness to pay is $1.49 + $0.20 − $0.10 = $1.59. Sally would be willing to pay up to $1.59 for our Del Monte beans.

Of course this is not exact. You will never know the true value that your customers put on your differentiation, but value accounting is invaluable as a framework and a way to think about these issues. Value accounting starts with how your customers make decisions and turns it around to provide an estimate of your customers' willingness to pay.

Internalizing value-based pricing is the most important thing you can do to have an impact on pricing at your company.

Describing value-based pricing as a process may make it look complicated. It isn't. Simply put, value-based pricing is determining how much your customer is willing to pay for your product. This willingness to pay depends on your competitor's price and the value of your differences.

Here are the steps to value-based pricing:

1. Identify your customer's second-best option to your product.
2. Determine the price of the second-best option.
3. List your advantages and disadvantages relative to the second-best option.
4. Estimate in dollars and cents the value of each advantage and disadvantage.
5. Calculate your price.

   Price of your product vs. the second-best option:
   + Value of advantages
   − Value of disadvantages
      Your calculated price

IMPACT PRICING

Simple. Well ... not really. The concept is simple. In practice this is a little more challenging.

All customers are different, so which one should you think about when doing this analysis? Choose a customer who purchased from you and do this analysis. Then choose a customer who didn't buy from you (harder to find to talk with) and do this analysis again. Customers who buy from you and those who don't value your offering differently. This is especially true for the value they place on your advantages and disadvantages. As a marketer your target audience should be the customers who value your advantages. Hence, you should price for those customers.

Doing the value-based pricing exercise with only one customer in mind does not provide the full picture. For situations where you set one price that many people see and use (TIOLI pricing), you'll want to do a value-based pricing exercise for several types of potential customers. Begin with the most typical customer and go through the entire process. After you've completed the exercise, do it again with a different customer type. For now we are assuming only one market segment. When you begin segmenting your pricing you will want to perform value-based pricing exercises for each segment. Part Two discusses customer segmentation.

Value-based pricing applies to most customer choices, not just physical products. When a customer is deciding which lawn service to hire, he will likely compare the attributes and the prices of several alternatives. If you run a lawn service, you'll want to know about your competitors, how you differ, and how your potential customers value those differences. Value-based pricing applies when choosing how or where to purchase a product, for example online or at a store. I'm probably not the only person to struggle with the decision on whether to go to a brick-and-mortar store like Best Buy or order online from Amazon.com. I compare the

Value-Based Pricing: Mandatory to Maximize Profits

convenience of not having to drive to the store, the amount of time I have to wait for the item, and the prices, including shipping and taxes. Every time a customer makes a choice based partially on price, value-based pricing is the way to think about the decision.

Let's look at each of the steps in more detail.

Identify Your Customer's Second-Best Option

> I use nothing but the best ingredients. My cookies are always baked fresh. I price cookies so that you cannot make them at home for any less.
>
> —Debbi Fields

#impactpricing

What will your customer choose if he or she doesn't choose you? This is his or her second-best option.

You have many competitors, and it's difficult to figure out which is truly the second-best option. To win the business, you have to have a better price for the value you offer than every competitor *that your customers will consider.* You know your competition, but verify it from your customers' and potential customers' points of view. Ask them what they would purchase if they didn't purchase from you.

List all of your competitors and rank order them based on how often your customers compare you to them. You only have to beat the competitors that your customers consider. Your customers do not always know all of the alternatives.

Do the value-based pricing exercise for several of the competitors toward the top of the list and for any competitors on the list that you consider especially challenging to compete against. Although your customer may not always consider your toughest competitors, when you can win against them you have a competitive advantage and should be able to grow revenue.

IMPACT PRICING

Determine the Price of the Second-Best Option

In this step it's important to include *all* relevant prices that your customer considers. For example, when I'm deciding between Best Buy and Amazon.com, I add in sales tax to the Best Buy alternative and shipping to the Amazon.com alternative. Not all people consider these costs, but if you're doing the analysis for me as a customer you would include sales tax and shipping. Whatever prices the customer is going to use when making the choice are the ones you need to use in your analysis.

The other side is to *only* use prices the customer will consider. One example is that airlines are now charging extra fees for checked baggage. However, most people don't use this in their choice decision because it's too difficult. Rather, they go to Expedia.com and compare the prices, which do not include baggage fees. So, if you were doing a value-based pricing exercise for air travel you would not include the baggage fees. If (when) Expedia or another travel site adds the ability to include these fees, then consumers will likely consider them as well when making their choice of flights. Then you would want to include them in your analysis. The point is that you want to use whatever prices your customers use when comparing your product to your competitor's.

> I need to know the price of a gallon of milk and a dozen eggs, and I need to know right now.
>
> —Lamar Alexander

#impactpricing

Finding your competitor's price sounds easy, but it's sometimes very challenging. In B2C situations, the consumer price is almost always published. After all, in a TIOLI market your competitor has to tell your customers what price it's charging. However, in B2B situations, where deals are individually negotiated, it's often difficult to learn how much your competitor really charges.

Value-Based Pricing: Mandatory to Maximize Profits

In these negotiated markets, you must estimate your competitors' prices. The easiest way to do that is feedback from your customers. Frequently your customers will tell you, after you've won or lost, what your competitor was charging. Sometimes your buyers will tell you early in the process that your competitor's price is much lower than yours. Be careful, this may be a poker maneuver to get you to lower your price. Some buyers lie about your competitors' prices. Some buyers don't tell you anything. What can work well in these situations is a competitor pricing database, a centralized competitor price repository. Anyone exposed to a competitor price would send it to the central location, and anyone who needs to know what competitors are charging can see the historical data. It's not perfect, but it's better than nothing.

List Your Advantages and Disadvantages Relative to the Second-Best Option

> Spend a lot of time talking to customers face to face. You'd be amazed how many companies don't listen to their customers.
> —Ross Perot

#impactpricing

Be thorough on this step. All you're doing is listing what's different between your product and your competitor's. If your customers don't value the differences, you'll account for that in the next step. For now, just list everything you can think of.

Make sure you consider the entire offering. This includes every nonproduct item that a customer may use when comparing two choices. For example, if you're a Ford dealer and want to price your Taurus relative to a Toyota Camry, you will certainly list the important features of the vehicles like engine size, fuel efficiency, roominess, etc. But if one of you has a special financing rate, then that needs to be included, too.

IMPACT PRICING

An often-overlooked differentiation is brand. Many companies spend millions of dollars building a brand, and that brand has value. On *Business Week*'s 2010 best global brands, Coca-Cola tops the list. Is there really a difference between Coke and RC Cola? Or Coke and Safeway Select Cola? There are certainly some differences, but in blind taste tests some people prefer RC or Safeway Select. Why does Coke receive a premium? It's their brand. People are willing to pay more for the Coke brand, but how much more? That's the topic of the next section.

> ### Differentiated Vodka?
>
> A walk down the vodka aisle at Beverages and More is a wonderful demonstration of brand. Stolichnaya Elit Vodka sells for $59.99 for 750 ml, Grey Goose Vodka is $26.98, and Nordic Star Vodka costs $7.99 for the same size. This doesn't seem unusual until you read Section 5.22 of the U.S. government's Standards of Identity for Distilled Spirits which defines vodka as "neutral spirits so distilled, or so treated after distillation with charcoal or other materials, as to be without distinctive character, aroma, taste, or color." In other words, by law you should not be able to tell one vodka from another. In this case (or bottle) it really may all be in the brand.

#impactpricing

Besides the product attributes, financing, and brand listed above, there are many more things that your customers may use. A partial list includes: the ease of doing business with you, your distribution channel, the quality of the reviews online, the number of other users, any word-of-mouth referrals, if there was a free trial, and more. All these and more are benefits that may have value to your customers that they may be willing to pay for. So anything you can think of that your customer considers when making their choices should go on your list.

Estimate in Dollars the Value of Each Advantage and Disadvantage

This is hard. Not only is it subjective, it's difficult to convince a marketer to be honest about this. Marketers spend their days thinking about why their product is the best, emphasizing the importance of their advantages, minimizing the importance of their competitors' advantages. Suddenly we are asking them to be completely unbiased. I've sat in meeting after meeting with marketers overemphasizing their own product's benefits and value. It's not intentional; it's simply the way they think.

Sometimes we have no choice but to rely on our marketers' opinions. However, there are many techniques we can use to get a second, possibly more accurate opinion.

One method is to ask your customers. This isn't completely accurate either. Your customers may not know how much they value certain features, or they may tell you they value them less than they do in an attempt to mislead you. Although it isn't perfect, it's another data point.

There are several statistical techniques you can incorporate in the right situations. One common method is called conjoint analysis, where a market researcher has customers make choices between fictional products with different sets of attributes. Using statistics they can tease out the value in dollars of each attribute. You can determine the value of certain channel attributes like end aisle display, a special discount, or a weekly flyer by analyzing scanner data from a retail outlet. Pricing consultants each have their own methods. For instance, Simon, Kucher and Partners employ a tool called ComStrat where marketers systematically estimate the importance and rating of each differentiating attribute.

Don't panic. The good news is no matter which method(s) you use, the results are not exact. It's important, though, to do the exercise for several reasons. First, the act of putting

IMPACT PRICING

a dollar value on your differentiable features emphasizes that your value comes from your differentiation. Second, the act of doing this step, of having all the marketers do this step, motivates everyone to start thinking about how they can add value. Finally, even if the results aren't perfect, as you set prices and talk with more customers, you will discern what's really important to your customers and how they're making their decisions. You'll be able to tweak your prices and, more important, your product offerings to better meet your customers' desires and create more value.

Calculate Your Price

Now that you've gone through the above steps, you have the price of the second-best option, and you have the value in dollars of each of the attributes that differentiate your offering and your competitors. The math is simple. Start with your competitor's price, add the dollar value of all attributes where you have the advantage, and subtract the dollar value of all of the attributes where your competitor is better. That's it. You now have a price.

If only it were that easy.

Unfortunately, when you get through the math you come up with a specific number, say, 43. That number is the price for the customer: whose second-best option is the one you chose, who sees the price that you started with for your competition, who values the attributes the same way you did. And even then, that price is the one that makes the customer indifferent between buying your product and the second-best option.

Obviously, 43 isn't the answer. However, it's probably in the ballpark. You may have calculated this assuming your toughest competitor. You don't always compete against that company, so maybe you should move the price up a little for when you compete against the easier ones. Or, you may be

Value-Based Pricing: Mandatory to Maximize Profits

chasing a broader market and you considered the customer that's ideal for your set of features, so maybe you should move the price down a little to capture value from other customers. Value-based pricing gets you close. You have to tweak this price up or down based on your judgment and experience.

Although value-based pricing does not give you the exact price, the thought process can and should drive decision making throughout the company. Possibly the biggest advantage to using value-based pricing throughout the company is it focuses minds to think about how the customer is going to choose between your product and another. Once you know about value-based pricing, it's obvious, but you'd be surprised at how many people don't understand this relatively simple concept. Charge what the customer is willing to pay.

Summary

Pricing a product using value-based pricing requires five steps:

1. Identify your customer's second-best option to your product.
2. Determine the price of the second-best option.
3. List your advantages and disadvantages relative to the second-best option.
4. Estimate in dollars the value of each advantage and disadvantage.
5. Calculate your price.

The result of this exercise is an actual price, which is most likely approximately correct, but still requires judgment on your part.

Throughout the chapter we emphasized that this is not exact. The process produces a precise number, but it is not accurate. The result depends on many subjective decisions you made during the exercise. Even though the price isn't perfect, there are two reasons to use value-based pricing. First, it gets you close. Second, and more important, it provides the framework for how everyone in the company can think about creating and capturing value. This value-based pricing exercise forces you and your colleagues to think critically about how your customers are making their decisions. Using value-based pricing you must identify and place a value on your differentiation. Differentiation creates value.

Summary Questions

- ✔ Think of a single product you offer. Who is your toughest competitor?
- ✔ Whom do you compete with most often?
- ✔ How much do these two (one?) competitors charge?
- ✔ Do you have a method to collect and share competitor prices?
- ✔ What are all the features and attributes that are different between you and these two competitors?
- ✔ Think of a single customer. How much does this customer value each of the things that are different?
- ✔ What price(s) does the value-based pricing math suggest you charge?

Actions: What are you going to do?

Chapter 5

Create Value:
Let Pricing Guide You

Business is not financial science, it's about trading ... buying and selling. It's about creating a product or service so good that people will pay for it.

—Anita Roddick

Key Concepts

- ✔ Real value comes from differentiation. Make value-based pricing part of product development.
- ✔ Marketing must create the perceived value.
- ✔ Influencing how your customers think about your competition affects your perceived value.

Pricing captures value. Everything else either creates value or destroys it.

That "everything else" is why you are in business, to create value for your customers. The products you sell, the services you bundle, the people you hire are almost completely dedicated to creating value. Most of your company's

IMPACT PRICING

energy is and should be focused on creating value. It is more difficult to create value than capture it.

This chapter analyzes value-based pricing from the perspective of helping you create more value. Now that you know how customers make decisions and how to use value-based pricing to capture more of the value you create, you can use this knowledge to help you do it even better.

> There are two functions, and two functions only, of any business: innovation and marketing.
> —Peter Drucker

#impactpricing

Although pricing can only capture the value you create, a thorough understanding of value-based pricing enables you to create more value, both real and perceived. Think deeply about the steps involved in value-based pricing, and you'll discover actions that can influence how much your customers are willing to pay for your product. This chapter discusses five of these methods.

Create Real Value with Differentiation

> You've got to look for a gap, where competitors in a market have grown lazy and lost contact with the readers or the viewers.
> —Rupert Murdoch

#impactpricing

Differentiation, differentiation, differentiation. Value is differentiation. If value-based pricing tells you anything it should tell you to build products and services that are different from your competitors and more useful to your customers.

Eli Broad, a founder of Kauffman and Broad (now KB Home), emphasized this point with the following statement. "At a time when all the other builders were selling homes with basements but without carports, we would sell homes

Create Value: Let Pricing Guide You

without basements and with carports. This allowed us to provide a more appealing product at a lower price. In other words, we felt we would be giving customers greater value." What he really did was build a home that was different. Some people may prefer a basement, but other people preferred a carport. By building a home differentiated by having a carport and a lower price, he was building more value for some homebuyers.

You won't please everyone. Don't even try. Create a product or service that's unique and meets the needs of some people. Value-based pricing gives you the opportunity to capture the value of your differentiation to these customers.

> Customers don't always know what they want. The decline in coffee-drinking was due to the fact that most of the coffee people bought was stale, and they weren't enjoying it. Once they tasted Starbucks and experienced what we call "the third place" ... a gathering place between home and work where they were treated with respect ... they found we were filling a need they didn't know they had.
> —Howard Schultz

#impactpricing

You're already investing resources in product development. How can you do this better? One thought is to run through the value-based pricing exercise at various stages during product development. As the development efforts progress, you'll learn more about what your customers like, more about what your competitors are doing, and more ideas about what's possible and feasible. Revisiting value-based pricing gives you an opportunity to put the brakes on bad projects early but, most important, it emphasizes to the product development team that you must design in differentiation. Value comes from differentiation.

IMPACT PRICING

Increase Perceived Value

> I don't design clothes. I design dreams.
> —Ralph Lauren

#impactpricing

The previous section emphasized building products with differentiation to create real value. This section is all about marketing. You can create a perfect product, highly differentiated from your nearest competition, and if your customers don't know about it, you can't price for it. This is what perceived value is all about.

Do your prospects know about your differentiation? Talk to them. If they don't know, then you need to improve your marketing. Your product development team spent time building in product differentiation, be sure to communicate this to your potential customers. Only then can you capture this value with a higher price.

> When the product is right, you don't have to be a great marketer.
> —Lee Iacocca

#impactpricing

Real value becomes perceived value when your customers know about it and value it. In the world of mass media, you will want to pick the most salient attribute to your target audience and push it hard. It's difficult to break through the clutter of mass media, to get someone's attention. But when you do get their attention, make sure your message is consistent and increases perceived value by emphasizing the extra benefits of your offering.

> Many a small thing has been made large by the right kind of advertising.
> —Mark Twain

#impactpricing

Earlier we discussed the value of a brand name (Coke) in

Create Value: Let Pricing Guide You

your customers' decisions. Their willingness to pay more for a brand name is perceived value. Peter Drucker says, "Suppliers and especially manufacturers have market power because they have information about a product or a service that the customer does not and cannot have, and does not need if he can trust the brand. This explains the profitability of brands." What he is saying is if you build a brand, your customers do less attribute-by-attribute comparison and place value instead on your brand name. Are you working on your brand?

> Creative things have to sell to get acknowledged as such. Steve Jobs didn't really set the direction of my Apple I and Apple II designs but he did the more important part of turning them into a product that would change the world.
>
> —Steve Wozniak

#impactpricing

Another idea is to make sure your direct sales force has access to all the information you generated in your value-based pricing exercise. Imagine your sales guy sitting in front of a major customer and that customer is comparing you to a specific competitor. You perform your value-based pricing exercise and document the differences between your product and that of your competitor, then give that information to your salesperson. You've now armed him or her with the knowledge of which features and benefits to push and which ones will not be of interest to the customer.

One of my favorite academic articles is titled "Meaningful Brands from Meaningless Differentiation: The Dependence on Irrelevant Attributes" by Gregory S. Carpenter, Rashi Glazer. and Kent Nakamoto. In this article they demonstrated that marketing an attribute, even if it is not differentiated, can add value. They used the example of Folgers coffee. What do you know about Folgers? You may remember that it is mountain grown. What you may not know is that all coffee is mountain grown. Folgers has advertised mountain grown enough that

IMPACT PRICING

we all think it's important. The lesson to take away is even if you haven't built in value with real differentiation, your marketing team can still create perceived value.

> Give the public everything you can give them, keep the place as clean as you can keep it, keep it friendly.
> —Walt Disney

#impactpricing

So far we've only talked about your marketing team and how they can create perceived value. If you want to build and capture a lot of perceived value, then get your entire company involved. Every customer touch point is a place to add or subtract value. Do you have a real person answering the phone? Are your customer service people friendly? Are your facilities clean? Everything and everybody your customer touches or sees either adds or subtracts value. Make sure it adds value.

> Make your product easier to buy than your competition, or you will find your customers buying from them, not you.
> —Mark Cuban

#impactpricing

Talk to your customers. Ask them what they like about doing business with you. Ask what they don't like. The answers they give you are their perception of your value. If you don't like the answers, get both your marketing team and your entire company involved in creating more perceived value.

Influence the Second-Best Option

USPS Express Mail is a letter delivered in one or two days and costs $2.95. Is that expensive or cheap? Remember your answer and then see below.

In the late 1990s the U.S. Postal Service ran a commer-

Create Value: Let Pricing Guide You

> ### Destroying Value
>
> In March 2011 Seth Godin wrote a blog post titled "Cascade of Broken Promises." In it he described a series of broken promises while resolving a problem with an Apple product called Migration Assistant. One instance was when someone told Seth he would receive a call back in less than 30 minutes. Over an hour later Seth still hadn't been called back. If you read Seth's blog you will know he is an Apple fan, so this was not a rant on Apple. He was making the point that it is so much easier to make a promise than to keep one. I use his story to make a different point: Every customer touch point either creates value or destroys it. This is an example of careless actions destroying value. Where is your company destroying value?

#impactpricing

cial that was fascinating to pricing geeks. A man comes on the screen, holds up an envelope and says "Federal Express will ship this to its destination in one day for $10.95. UPS will ship this to its destination in one day for $9.95. With U.S. Postal Service Express Mail it will get there in one or two days for only $2.95."

The brilliance of this commercial is that it was influencing your second-best option. Recall your answer to the question of was $2.95 cheap or expensive. If you thought it was cheap you were probably already comparing this to FedEx or UPS. But if you thought it was expensive you were likely comparing it to the 44 cent price of the stamp required to mail a letter for two- or three-day delivery.

This is an example of how you can influence which competitors your potential customer uses to compare, which in turn effects how much he is willing to pay. Another example, not quite as clever, is car ads. We frequently see cars like Hyundai comparing themselves to cars like Lexus.

If your product is enough out of the mainstream, then you may be able to influence the choice of the second-best option simply by putting out your own comparison charts, showing how you are almost as good as a much more expensive alternative.

Influence the Perceived Price of the Second-Best Option

The value-based pricing math begins with the price of your competitor's product. What price will your prospect use? You may be able to influence this perceived price.

This is most common when your competitor advertises or shows a low price, but you know there are hidden fees and expenses on top. Southwest Airlines used this technique with their "Bags Fly Free" campaign. Consumers tend to use the prices they see on Expedia or Travelocity to choose their flights. But these prices don't include baggage fees while Southwest fares include free checked luggage. With the "Bags Fly Free" campaign Southwest was attempting to make these other airlines appear more expensive by emphasizing the hidden fees.

Some companies use this technique when emphasizing total cost of ownership or the perceived costs of using a product. For example, Whole Foods has a blog post titled "Why Quick, Cheap Food Is More Expensive Than You Think." In this post they reference another article that outlined the costs and causes of obesity in the United States. This is an obvious attempt to make their wholesome, fresh, and expensive food appear more affordable.

Are there hidden costs in your competitor's offering that your potential customers are ignoring? If so, you may want to point them out.

Use Price to Signal Quality

This is a special case of creating perceived value. In many cases shoppers don't know the quality of products or services before they purchase them. In these cases, they tend to use price as an indicator of which one is better. They are proba-

Create Value: Let Pricing Guide You

bly thinking something like, "After all, other people pay those prices, and they can't all be wrong, can they?" Or they may be thinking, "The shop owner knows what he's doing and would of course charge more for the better products." Or they may not be thinking at all and are in the habit of paying more for higher quality—you get what you pay for. Regardless, they certainly do use the price as a piece of information indicating how good a product or service is.

> You get what you pay for.

#impactpricing

A classic example is wine. It's impossible to tell the quality of a wine without tasting it. Wine reviewers give ratings to wines, which is a data point we can use to predict the quality. But if you see a $20 bottle of wine rated 92 by Parker right next to an unrated bottle at $40, which do you think is better? I vote for the $40 bottle. Studies show that even sommeliers (professional wine tasters), while doing a blind tasting with price as the only piece of additional information, use price to color their ratings.

Many services follow this rule as well. It is difficult to sample different attorneys when you have to go to court. If you are falsely accused of murder would you rather have a $300/hour attorney or a $500/hour attorney? I know which one I would choose.

However, price is rarely the sole indicator of quality. Imagine a guy pulls up to your house in a minivan with a magnetic sticker on the door that says "Bob's Wines." He opens the side door and shows you several cases of wine with homemade labels on them and tells you they are $50 per bottle. Do you think they're quality? Probably not. Or imagine an attorney, 26 years old, fresh out of law school, working out of his apartment, charging $500 per hour. Do you think he's worth it? Again, probably not. This means

IMPACT PRICING

you can't simply raise prices and get everyone to think your offerings are high quality. However, when these other indicators of quality are the same or similar across options, price becomes the default attribute used to judge quality.

Price works phenomenally well as a signal of quality for products where it's challenging for the shopper to determine a more subjective measure. However, because consumers are lazy and won't do the work to fully evaluate their options, price can signal quality in many other situations, as well.

Of course, raising your price may mean you sell less of your product because fewer people will think it's worth it to them. Think very carefully before raising prices significantly enough in the hope that people will think your offering is higher quality. A better option might be to add higher-end products to your portfolio, but more on that in a later chapter.

Summary

> It's an interesting way to think about marketing. Is your product better than it sounds, or does it sound better than it is? We call the first a discovery, something worthy of word of mouth. The second? Hype.
> —Seth Godin

#impactpricing

When you play a game of chess or checkers, you think several moves ahead and then work backwards to make your best decision. While developing new products, thinking ahead to pricing is like thinking several moves ahead. That perspective may guide you to better decisions.

Using value-based pricing, we charge for perceived value. The key question for this chapter is "How can we generate more perceived value?"

It starts with real differentiation. Introducing value-based pricing early into the new product development process provides a constant reminder to differentiate. Value

Create Value: Let Pricing Guide You

comes from differentiation. Then real value is turned into perceived value through marketing. Customers only value the differences they know. Talk to your customers to learn what they're aware of. You may be able to increase perceived value by influencing which competitor your prospects compare you to and the price these prospects use for your competitor in comparison to your offering. Make sure your customers know about competitors' hidden fees and costs. Finally, you may want to use a higher price just to influence the perceived quality of your offering.

As a company, your objective is to create value for your customers. Value-based pricing provides a framework to help you do it.

Summary Questions

- ✔ How early in the new product definition stage does your product development team focus on differentiation?
- ✔ How often do they revisit differentiation?
- ✔ Are you sharing this differentiation information systematically with your sales force?
- ✔ Do your customers know about your differentiation?
- ✔ Which competitors would you like your customers to use when comparing you?
- ✔ Are there any hidden fees or costs in doing business with your competitors?
- ✔ Is it easy for your customers to judge quality before purchasing?

Actions: What are you going to do?

Costs Matter:
But Not How You Think

The essence of a successful business is really quite simple. It is your ability to offer a product or service that people will pay for at a price sufficiently above your costs, ideally three or four or five times your cost, thereby giving you a profit that enables you to buy and to offer more products and services.

—Brian Tracy

Key Concepts

- ✔ Fixed costs are irrelevant to pricing.
- ✔ Variable costs are important when defining the floor to accept negotiated deals.
- ✔ Variable costs are important in finding the profit-maximizing price for TIOLI markets.
- ✔ Standard costs can lead to bad decisions.
- ✔ Cost-plus pricing is easy, but not optimal.
- ✔ Pay attention to observable costs.

IMPACT PRICING

If you aren't an accountant, you're probably thinking, "Please pull my teeth so I don't have to read a chapter on costs." There may not be a more boring topic in pricing than costs. Unfortunately, costs matter when making pricing decisions, and most people use costs incorrectly. Even pricing professionals get this wrong.

In an attempt to make this dry subject interesting, I will attempt to suprise you in each section with examples of bad decisions that happen when costs aren't used correctly. Hopefully you'll avoid these errors.

Before starting, it's important to realize the answer to "which costs matter?" differs for TIOLI markets and negotiated markets. As a quick reminder, TIOLI markets (take it or leave it) are the prices used in the grocery store and most consumer markets. The seller puts a single price on an item, and the customer decides whether or not to purchase it. There is no negotiation.

In negotiated markets, every transaction is negotiated. For example, Google negotiates with storage suppliers when expanding or building new data centers. The price Google pays is likely different from the price Yahoo! or Amazon.com or eBay pays. We covered this in Chapter 2, which you can refer to for a review.

Fixed Costs Are Irrelevant to Pricing

Two companies, A and B, design software games. Players (customers) like the two games equally and have the same willingness to pay. If Company A spent $10M on product development and Company B spent $1M on product development, should Company A charge a higher price?

No. The players do not know or even care about the development costs. The players only care if they like it and how much it costs. The development costs, like all fixed costs, are irrelevant to pricing.

Costs Matter: But Not How You Think

It's true. Your fixed costs are not relevant to your pricing decisions.

If you believe in value-based pricing, then your price should be determined by how much your customers are willing to pay. Their willingness to pay is driven by the amount of value they perceive for your product. That value is determined by what else they would do with their money and the incremental benefit your product or service provides. Their willingness to pay does not change if you have higher R&D costs. Their willingness to pay does not change if you double your staff. Your fixed costs do not matter at all to your customers' willingness to pay, and therefore they should not matter in your pricing decisions.

> Drucker said, 'If you weren't already in this business, would you enter it today? And if not, what are you going to do about it?' ... Simple, right? But incredibly powerful.
> —Jack Welch

#impactpricing

Many misconceptions revolve around how to use fixed costs in pricing. I've heard pricing consultants advise that past fixed costs (i.e., sunk costs) don't matter, but future fixed costs do. *Wrong.* What matters to pricing is the amount of value you offer and your customer's willingness to pay (and variable costs as you'll see in the next section).

Fixed costs *do* matter, just not to pricing. Fixed costs matter when you decide whether to get into a business. Take for example Electronic Arts (EA) and their Madden NFL '11 game. They've spent millions of dollars developing this game, especially considering this is a continuation of many previous versions. Those millions of dollars are all sunk costs and they don't matter to anything. The only thing they can do is attempt to recapture those development costs by selling lots of copies of this game. So far EA has sold almost 6 million units of Madden NFL '11 so they've likely made a profit.

IMPACT PRICING

Should EA spend a few million more dollars to develop Madden NFL '12? The answer is determined by estimating how many units they can sell. Let's assume they can sell another 6 million units if they release Madden NFL '12. The retail price is $59.95, but that is what Best Buy receives, not EA. Let's estimate that EA receives less than half of that or $25 per unit when selling into their distribution channel. We can also estimate their cost of manufacturing (variable cost) is around $5. Their gross profit per unit is the price they sell to their distribution channel minus their variable costs which we now estimate that to be around $20 per unit. Our rough estimates of 6 million units times $20 per unit show that EA can bring in about $120M in gross profit. Should they spend a few more million in development costs? Absolutely.

Fixed costs are not used to determine the optimal price. As we see in this example though, our estimates of the optimal price, the amount we can sell, and the fixed costs determine whether we should undertake the project. This same calculation is made over and over again in every company. Can you make enough gross profit using optimal pricing to exceed your fixed costs? Which projects should the company invest in? That is the decision in which fixed costs matter.

Variable Costs Are Relevant

What is the role of variable cost in pricing? It depends on if you are pricing for a TIOLI or negotiated market.

Let's discuss the easy one first, the negotiated market. Purchasing agents for large companies often demand the right to negotiate individual purchases. In these situations, the price one customer pays is not directly related to the price any other customer pays. The buyer is seeking to negotiate the best deal for his organization, and your salesperson is negotiating the best deal for your company. In these negotiated deals, variable costs play only one role: They address the question, "Do you want to accept this piece of business?"

Costs Matter: But Not How You Think

Your salesperson negotiates the best price he or she can get from the customer. This is your customer's willingness to pay for this transaction. The only decision left to make is do you want this piece of business?

You may think you can go back with another price, and you may be able to. That's still part of the negotiation process. When you have the best deal you can make with this customer, your only decision is whether to accept the business. Do you want to accept it? If the price is below your variable costs then the answer is almost certainly no. There would need to be a strategic reason to accept a deal below your variable costs.

This doesn't mean you accept all business above variable costs. There may be reasons not to. Possibly your investors have margin expectations that you need to hit. You may not want to devalue your product to others if they find out the low price you gave to one customer. You may not want your channel to see such a low price. Regardless, you certainly would not accept business below variable costs without some good strategic reasons. The role of variable costs in negotiated markets is to help determine whether to accept a piece of business.

In TIOLI markets variable costs play a more direct role in pricing. When companies change prices, they change the number of units they sell. Most of the time when you raise your price you will sell fewer units. If you could estimate the number of units you sell at every price point, you can create a demand curve. With an accurate demand curve it's easy to determine the optimal price using math and/or graphs. Many pricing books or exercises assume you can determine your demand curve. However, I've never seen a company that really knows its demand curve.

Instead, let's think about this problem in increments. Should you raise (or lower) your price by some relatively small amount? If you raise your price, you'll make more money per unit, but sell fewer units. Should you do it? First calculate your current gross profit:

Gross Profit = Quantity Sold x (Price − Variable Cost)

Then select the new price you are considering and estimate the quantity you'll sell at the new price. Calculate your new gross profit. If the estimated gross profit at the new price is higher than at the current price, then raise prices.

Two things to notice. (1) Variable costs are part of the above process. Variable costs matter. (2) Fixed costs are not found anywhere in the calculation. Fixed costs do not matter.

> The surest foundation of a manufacturing concern is quality. After that, and a long way after, comes cost.
> —Andrew Carnegie

#impactpricing

There's a fine line between costs that are fixed and costs that are variable. One way to think about this is to ask, "What is the cost of building one more unit?" In many cases this is only the cost of materials, since you will likely not be hiring someone to build the next unit, or you won't need a new piece of equipment or even a new factory. However, in some cases you may be thinking if you lower prices a little you could sell a lot more. In this case you will want to add the incremental fixed costs into your analysis. These decisions are best made using spreadsheets and modeling the outcomes under different assumptions.

To summarize, variable costs do matter. They either influence the floor at which we are willing to accept negotiated business, or they directly impact the profit maximizing price in TIOLI markets.

Standard Costs Can Be a Mistake

Many companies calculate a "standard cost" by allocating their total manufacturing overhead (fixed costs) to individual

Costs Matter: But Not How You Think

> **Cost of Consulting**
>
> Independent consultants are an interesting case study on costs. What are their costs? Let's focus only on their labor costs and how they apply to pricing. If they believe they are worth $100 per hour then they might say their variable costs are $100 per hour. But this isn't true. If they are only working 20 hours per week, what is their incremental cost in working another hour? If we are only considering labor, it's $0. Accepting a job at $50 per hour may be preferable to starving. If however, the consultant is paying an employee to work at $20 per hour and pays that person only for billable hours, then she really does have a variable cost of $20. If she pays that person whether the hours are billed or not, then the costs are fixed and are not relevant to her pricing decisions.

#impactpricing

products. For example, if a company has $2 million overhead and it forecasts that it will sell 1 million units, then they allocate $2 of fixed costs to each unit. This is fine for accounting purposes, but not for pricing. It can cause bad business decisions, especially for relatively low-margin products. For example, imagine this company with the $2 million of fixed costs and 1 million units. Also, imagine that their variable costs are only $0.10. If we allocate the fixed costs then their standard costs are $2.10 ($2 fixed costs plus $0.10 variable cost).

Now, the salesperson finds a new opportunity, one the company didn't expect, didn't forecast. Maybe it's in a completely different market. This new customer wants to purchase 100,000 units but will only pay $1.90. They can sell 100,000 incremental units if they are willing to sell them for $1.90. Should they accept it?

Since $1.90 is below their standard costs, the easy answer is no. Why would any company sell below costs? This is the problem with standard costs. If they instead use true variable costs they would be comparing $1.90 to $0.10, which sounds like a great deal. Of course life is never this simple. There may be other reasons to turn down this business, like they don't want this price to be seen in the market. The key takeaway, though, is allocating fixed costs can lead us to bad pricing and business decisions.

However, using standard costs can have a positive impact on pricing, as well. In large companies many people are involved in pricing decisions for a given opportunity. Using standard cost as the cost floor and then a margin goal on top of that is a more conservative approach. This makes employees reluctant to lower prices too much, which at least partially counters the additional sales pressure to lower prices.

Here is a suggestion for large companies on how to handle standard vs. variable costs. Go ahead and use standard costs for the majority of your pricing decisions. However, when you've defined your escalation process as to who has to approve the exceptional low-margin deals, make sure the final decision maker is using true variable costs in their decision.

Observable Costs

Let's take a couple of paragraphs to point out a special type of cost. An *observable cost* is a variable cost that your customers typically know. A common example is the price of fuel to the airline industry.

The reason observable costs are important is that customers *hate* price increases, which you will read more about in Chapter 15. They especially hate price increases when they think you are just making more profit on them. Yet customers are more forgiving when you are "passing along" your own price increases. To do this, you will want to know which of your costs your customers know about, and use those as reasons for raising prices. The airline industry is a classic, raising seat prices and fees whenever fuel prices jump up.

Costs Matter: But Not How You Think

Cost-Plus Pricing

Cost-plus pricing seems to be the most commonly used pricing technique in business today. After all, cost-plus pricing is easy to implement, it ensures you are making a reasonable margin, it makes competing predictable, and it's seen as fair to all of your customers. Unfortunately, it leaves a lot of money on the table.

Easy to implement. Once you've decided on your desired margin, you simply multiply your variable costs times a markup to get your price. For example, if you want a 50 percent margin, you multiply your variable costs times 2. If you want 66 percent margin you multiply costs times 3. This is especially beneficial when you have many products and don't have the people to set individual prices.

Ensures a reasonable margin. By using the same markup on all products, you know that you are getting a specified margin. Firms with more complex pricing mechanisms may sometimes be selling products at low margins (think loss leader).

Competition is predictable. If both you and your competitors have a lot of products, it can be difficult to know how to price relative to your competition on every part. However, knowing that your competitor uses a standard markup enables you to also use a standard markup and remain consistently priced relative to your competition.

It's fair. Many businesspeople are uncomfortable charging different customers different prices or even charging different markups for different products. They feel it's not fair. Cost-plus pricing seems exceptionally fair.

There are probably other benefits to using cost-plus pricing, but cost-plus pricing *doesn't maximize your profits*. We've spent a lot of time talking about pricing according to how much customers are willing to pay. Value-based pricing maximizes your profits. Price to your customer's willingness to pay.

IMPACT PRICING

If you've read this far in the book, then you are likely convinced to use value-based pricing and will at least consider the pricing strategies derived from it. But how do you move away from cost-plus pricing (if you haven't already)?

Let me suggest you start with a modified cost-plus approach. Keep your current process, but find one customer segment that's willing to pay more and charge a higher margin to those customers. Or, if you have a good, better, best product family, raise the margin on the best. You will quickly see that there's a lot of money to be made by pricing based on customer value rather than your costs. Slowly add more segments or more techniques and soon you won't be looking back at cost-based pricing.

In the long run you may have a combination of cost-plus and value-based pricing. If you have a large portfolio of products, you may want to use cost-plus on the less important items, but use value-based pricing on the parts that generate the most revenue, profit, and growth.

Summary

Value-based pricing means charging customers what they are willing to pay. Your customer's willingness to pay does not depend on your costs. Unfortunately many companies put too much emphasis on their costs when making pricing decisions.

In value-based pricing, the only relevant costs are variable costs. For negotiated markets, variable costs help advise which business to accept or reject. For TIOLI markets, the variable costs are part of the gross profit per unit vs. number of units sold trade-off. So they must be considered.

Fixed costs are irrelevant to pricing. They matter a lot when deciding whether or not to get into a business or build a new product. But once that decision has been made, they become irrelevant. Some companies allocate fixed costs to

Costs Matter: But Not How You Think

products based on forecasted demand. Using these standard costs can lead to bad pricing decisions.

Costs may not be the most glamorous topic in pricing, but using them incorrectly can cause companies to make suboptimal decisions.

Summary Questions

- ✔ Does your company use standard costs or true variable costs?
- ✔ If you use standard costs, do you have someone in the escalation process who knows variable costs?
- ✔ What observable costs do you have?

Actions: What are you going to do?

Pricing Segmentation: The Most Profitable Strategies

Segment. Concentrate. Dominate.

—Don Tyson

Chapter 7

Introduction to Price Segmentation:
Rich and Poor

I think Amazon is the preeminent pioneer in building a new way of doing commerce: personalized, database-driven commerce, where the big value is not in the purchase fulfillment, but in knowing as much about a customer base of ten or twenty million people as a corner store used to know about a customer base of a few hundred. In today's mass-merchandising world, that's largely gone; Amazon is trying to use computer technology to re-establish it.

—Andrew Grove

Key Concepts

- ✔ Price segmentation allows you to capture some business at higher prices and simultaneously win incremental business at lower prices.
- ✔ There are two steps to price segmentation.
  - Identify the segments.
  - Create a separating mechanism.
- ✔ Price segmentation can be fair!

IMPACT PRICING

Price segmentation is the *most powerful* tool you have in your pricing toolbox. Every company, big or small, must be thinking about price segmentation.

Price segmentation is simply charging different prices to different people for the same or a similar product or service. You see examples every time you go shopping: student prices at movie theaters, senior prices for coffee at McDonald's, people who use coupons, and many more. One example of excellence in price segmentation is the airline industry. It seems that no two people traveling on the same plane paid the same price. Whether you're an airline, retailer, restaurant, software company, consultant, or building physical products, price segmentation applies to you.

Your goal is to capture more of the value you create. We saw in the chapter on value that different customers value your products differently. Different customers are willing to pay differing amounts for your product. Price segmentation is the mechanism that "allows" customers to pay an amount closer to their true willingness to pay.

Imagine for a second that you build a product for $25 cost. You have two types of customers, a segment that's willing to pay $100 and a segment that's willing to pay $75. How much do you charge? If you only get to set one price and everyone buys at the same price, then it depends on how large each segment is. If you charge $75 you can sell to everyone, but make less per unit. If you charge $100 you make more per unit, but the people who will only pay $75 won't purchase. What if you could charge the people willing to pay $75 that amount and you could charge those with a higher willingness to pay the full $100? Now you're maximizing profit.

If you currently charge all customers the same price, consider the following. There are likely some people who purchase your product who would have purchased it at a higher price. What if you could identify those people and get

Introduction to Price Segmentation: Rich and Poor

them to pay more without raising the price on everyone else? That would certainly add profit to your books. There are also likely some people who didn't buy from you but would have if the price had been just a little bit lower. What if you could identify those people and charge them less without lowering the prices for everyone else? Assuming these are still profitable customers, then again you've grown your bottom line.

This is what price segmentation can do for you. It can earn you higher average sales prices from your existing customers while capturing more customers at the lower end. Let's start segmenting.

How to Segment on Price

Price segmentation requires two steps: (1) Identify the segments and (2) create a separating pricing mechanism.

1. Identify the segments. The first requirement is to find groups of customers, some who are willing to pay more and others not willing to pay so much. To keep this simple, let's hold it to two segments, those willing to pay more and those who will only buy at a lower price. Let's call them the "rich" and the "poor." This is a pretty common segmentation. In general poor people are more willing to invest time, energy, and effort to get lower prices, while rich people don't want to spend extra effort and are willing to pay more not to do that.

2. Create a separating pricing mechanism. A separating mechanism is a technique or strategy that enables some customers to pay a lower price and requires others to pay a higher price. This is more difficult than it sounds. You can't simply put up a sign in your store that says "Rich people—$10; Poor people—$5." Although that is what we're trying to do, nobody would ever confess to being rich. You need a way to get the rich people to voluntarily pay the higher price. In some industries this is easy. When every customer gets quoted a unique price, you just need to figure out what price

IMPACT PRICING

to quote based on their segment. However, in most industries, especially in B2C settings, this is more challenging. You will learn many examples of how to do this including coupons, sales, and student IDs.

Let's look at the example of students at the movie theater. The movie industry has determined that most of us (nonstudents) are the "rich," and that students are the "poor." This may not be accurate, but in general it would be fair to say that students who don't have full-time jobs are less well off than those who work for a living. However, the movie industry wants both segments to come to the theaters so they charge students less to attract them. The separating pricing mechanism is to offer a discount to students who show their ID. That way most of us pay the normal price, and students get a lower price. Two segments, two prices.

The best way to learn price segmentation is to go through many different examples, which you will find in the next several chapters. As you read these examples, your goal should be to figure out which of these price segmentation methods can work for your company. Take each concept, stretch it and twist it, use it to inspire your creation of a new segmentation technique. There are four generic methods to segment your customers for pricing: customer characteristics, customer behaviors, transaction characteristics, and product characteristics. The first three of these are the next three chapters. The one on product characteristics is discussed in Chapter 12.

Is This Fair?

> The most important single central fact about a free market is that no exchange takes place unless both parties benefit.
> —Milton Friedman

#impactpricing

Conversations with customers, managers, and even pricers demonstrate that many people are uncomfortable with the

Introduction to Price Segmentation: Rich and Poor

concept of price segmentation. When asked the question, "Is it fair to charge two people different prices?" many people answer no. What do you think? Is it fair or is it cheating customers?

First, price segmentation is not cheating customers. You never force anybody to purchase from you. You are not being deceptive. You have to offer more value to the customer than you charge, or he will not purchase. In fact, every time customers purchase from you, they receive more value than they pay (otherwise they wouldn't buy from you). There is nothing unfair about this!

Second, when we change the wording of the question to, "Is it fair to charge students less to see a movie?" most people answer yes. And why wouldn't it be? You can find thousands of situations where companies charge customers different amounts, with nobody claiming they are being cheated.

Fair is in the mind of the beholder. Put yourself in your customers' shoes and ask how you would feel facing the prices that your company uses. If you would feel cheated, so would they. I was working with a couple of consultants who had the right idea but the wrong implementation. Before I ever talked with them, they knew they wanted to price their projects based on how much value their customers would receive. Every customer, every project could have a different price. Bravo! Then they described their implementation. "When a potential customer asks how much we charge, we tell them we have to determine how much value we can provide before quoting a price." Put yourself in their customer's shoes. They just told you that they are going to do their best to charge you as much as possible. A better answer would have been "We charge $500 as an hourly rate. For large projects we are willing to make a fixed bid proposal by estimating the amount of time required and multiplying that times a lower hourly rate of $400. However, if in the bidding process we find we cannot add as much value to you as we normally do, we may use an even lower rate. We want to make sure you receive far more value than your costs." Now the customer feels there is a fair process, even if he ends up paying the highest rates.

Fair really is in the mind of the beholder. We think something is unfair when it is both unexpected and not in our favor. For example, airlines have been charging different prices for seats on the same flight for a very long time, but we don't complain about the fairness of this practice. We know the rules, and we each play them the best we can. However, when airlines started charging a fee for checked baggage there was uproar. Travelers claimed the airlines are just gouging. However, once we all become used to the new rules, fairness will cease being an issue. After all, it wasn't that long ago that they stopped providing meals on planes unless you paid for them. That is no longer considered unfair.

Not only is price segmentation fair, it is beneficial to the less well off. If a movie theater could only charge one price to everyone, then they would probably just eliminate student pricing. Students, who tend to make less money, would see fewer movies. Eliminating price segmentation wouldn't help those of us who pay full price. It only hurts the people who can't pay that price.

Summary

This chapter is an introduction to price segmentation, emphasizing its importance. Most customers are different. They differ in their tastes, their needs, and their preferences. They also differ in their willingness to pay. Price segmentation allows you to capture more of each customer's willingness to pay. There are two steps to segmenting on price: identify segments with different willingness to pay and create a mechanism that allows you to charge the segments different prices.

Introduction to Price Segmentation: Rich and Poor

One of the biggest concerns about price segmentation is fairness. Is it fair? Considering we see it all around us, some implementations are certainly considered fair. Typically, the only time a customer thinks price segmentation is unfair is when it is unexpected and not in his or her favor.

Summary Questions

- ✔ Identify price segmentation techniques used in your industry. (This exercise will become easier after reading the next several chapters.)
- ✔ What are the segments?
- ✔ What is the separating mechanism?
- ✔ Are any of them unfair? Why?

Actions: What are you going to do?

Chapter 8

Customer Characteristics:
Who Are You?

Customers buy for their reasons, not yours.

—Orvel Ray Wilson

Key Concepts

✔ Identifiable characteristics about your customers may indicate their willingness to pay.

✔ Have a normally high price and ask customers to prove they deserve a discount.

Sometimes you're able to identify a characteristic about a customer that's correlated with the customer's willingness to pay. In these situations you can set different prices for each segment.

In some cases, you know which segment the customer is in. For example, in B2B you typically know what region your customer is in, and you may charge different prices based on geography. For age-based pricing, you may be able to estimate someone's age to tell if they are under 12 or over 65.

IMPACT PRICING

Yet in some cases you don't know the customer segment unless the customer volunteers that information. For example you can't tell if a young woman is a student unless she shows her student ID. In situations like these, you must offer an incentive for people to prove who they are. This is done by setting your normal or published price at the high level, targeting your customers with the higher willingness to pay. Then you offer a discount to the customers who prove to you they are in the price sensitive segment.

If you can identify some characteristic about your customers that correlates with their willingness to pay then you should be able to turn that into a price segmentation mechanism. Here are several examples.

Age

We already used the example of students getting a discount at the movie theater. Another common example here is senior citizens receiving discounts on coffee at McDonald's. Both the young and the old tend to be more price sensitive than those in their peak earning years. The pricing mechanism is that both groups carry some type of ID and are required to show it in order to get the discount. No ID, no discount.

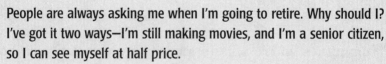

> People are always asking me when I'm going to retire. Why should I? I've got it two ways—I'm still making movies, and I'm a senior citizen, so I can see myself at half price.
>
> —George Burns

#impactpricing

Local vs. Tourist

Disneyland has a special price for an annual pass if you live in Southern California. The Taj Mahal in India offers an 80 percent discount to locals. Las Vegas casinos frequently have special pricing for buffets if you live in Las Vegas. In each of these cases locals have a lower willingness to pay

Customer Characteristics: Who Are You?

than tourists. To attract the locals, these companies offer special local pricing. The pricing mechanism is the requirement to show an ID with a local address on it in to get the discount.

Geography

In B2B it is common to charge different prices based on which region of the world the customer is located. Typically the Asia-Pacific region receives the lowest prices because companies there tend to be focused on producing at the lowest costs. If an American company was extremely focused on costs, they would probably move manufacturing to China. The pricing mechanism here is simple because companies typically know where their B2B customers are located and are able to charge each company a separately negotiated price. For B2B companies that use distributors around the world, they typically offer different prices to the distributors based on their location. There is commonly a different price list for each region.

Market Segment

In B2B it's common to charge different prices to customers in different market segments. For example, the medical market segment tends to be much more focused on quality than on price, so they are less price sensitive than, say, the consumer products market segment where price is a major driver. Similar to the geographical segmentation, companies typically know which market segment their customers are in. Negotiated pricing allows a different price for each customer.

Historical Purchase Behavior

In B2B, companies frequently have resale data for most of their end customers. This resale data includes what has been purchased in the past and at what prices. Some analysis of this data could directly characterize each customer by their willingness to pay. If some customers usually pay a higher price than most other customers, then they would be value buyers, meaning they are willing to pay for value. When they ask for a new quote, there is no need to give them your best price. However, a company that usually pays much less than most other customers is probably very price sensitive and works hard to make sure it gets the best price. Companies in this category are called price buyers and will likely end up with a low price.

Summary

Each of these segmentation methods is an example of identifying some characteristic about customers that is correlated with their willingness to pay and then using that information to determine the price they receive. In some markets, especially B2B, you can identify the customer characteristic and negotiate a unique price with each customer. In markets where you rely on customers to identify their segment, this only works when your normal price is for customers with the higher willingness to pay, and you provide incentive to the other group to "prove" they deserve a discount.

Here is another example that doesn't fit in the above categories. Put yourself in the shoes of a car salesman at a GM dealer. A customer walks in and wants to purchase a new Malibu. How would you determine how big of a discount you will need to give him? You may look to see what kind of car he currently drives, how nice the clothes are that he's wearing, or the brand of watch he has on. What kinds of questions did he ask? Were they more about the car or the price? These are all characteristics about the customer that provide hints about his willingness to pay. Although this chapter identified five characteristics that are frequently used in price segmentation, this car example shows there can be many more. Can you think of more?

Customer Characteristics: Who Are You?

Summary Questions

✔ How can you apply each one of these in your industry?
- Age
- Local vs. tourist
- Geography
- Market segment
- Historical purchase behavior

✔ Can you think of any other customer characteristics that may identify price sensitivity in your market?

Actions: What are you going to do?

Chapter 9

Customer Behaviors:
Jump This Hurdle

Consumers are statistics. Customers are people.

—Stanley Marcus

Key Concepts

✔ Your customers self-select into segments when you attach an obstacle to a lower price.

✔ Put up hurdles only price-sensitive customers will jump.

Segmenting prices through customer behavior is fascinating. Instead of identifying characteristics of your customers and then charging a price based on that characteristic, in this method you create different pricing mechanisms and your customers choose which ones to use. Their behaviors indicate their willingness to pay. When you do this well, the customers who are more price sensitive choose the lower price, and the ones who are less price sensitive choose the higher price.

In each of the following examples, customers who are

more price sensitive behave in ways different from those customers who are less price sensitive. Price-sensitive customers may be willing to put more time and effort into finding a good deal; they may be more patient waiting for a good deal; they may be more thorough in evaluating alternatives; they may use more foresight to strategically get the best prices; and they may even invest money up front in an effort to save money in the long run. What is fascinating about this type of price segmentation is that you don't have to know which customer is in which segment. You set up the separating pricing mechanism, and your customers self-select.

Henry David Thoreau said, "The price of anything is the amount of life you exchange for it." What each of these examples has in common is that we're asking our customers to invest both money and life. Life is in the form of time, energy, effort, patience, foresight, and more, all things we would rather not waste, but the more price sensitive among us will invest these to achieve a lower price.

These pricing mechanisms all have one thing in common, there is a hurdle put in place that price-sensitive customers must jump over to get a lower price. Customers who are willing to pay more are not willing to jump that hurdle.

Coupons (Effort)

Coupons are a common way to implement segmented pricing. People who are willing to invest the time and energy to get a lower price will look for, clip, and use coupons. People who are less price sensitive will not clip coupons, so they pay more. This segmentation is not black and white. Very few people always use coupons, and most of us would be willing to use a coupon if it was worth enough. For example, most of us do not use coupons to save a dollar off of Welch's Grape Juice, but I would wager that most of us would be willing to use a coupon for 50 percent off of a new car. Right now on the Internet there are hundreds of sites that offer coupons

Customer Behaviors: Jump This Hurdle

you can use. Do you use them? If not, why not? Probably because most of us are not that price sensitive. Think about who uses those sites ... people who are price sensitive, people who are willing to put in the effort to get a better deal.

> **Coupons for the Community Conscious**
>
> This technique has been used successfully by small local retail stores like pizza restaurants or pottery studios. Enlist a local community organization like a Boy Scout troop or an elementary school. Have coupons printed up for say 10 percent off plus 10 percent goes to the community organization. Now you've "hired" a community group to help you market. This community group will find potential customers who are sympathetic to their group and helping that group adds more value to your product for those customers.

#impactpricing

Rebates (Effort)

Rebates are similar to coupons, only better. The big advantage to a rebate is that customers who did not put in the effort to look for a coupon can decide to take advantage of a rebate advertised at the point of purchase. Then, a large portion of these customers, who used the rebate in their purchase decision, will not fill out the rebate forms. This is like promising a discount without having to live up to the promise. Only the truly price-sensitive customers actually request their rebates. Think about your own behavior. Have you ever used the rebate price in your purchase decision but then failed to send in the rebate form?

Sales Events (Patience)

Brooks Brothers is a higher-end classic men's clothing store. They don't have very many sales, so most of the time when you go in their store, you will pay their normal price. However, a few times a year they have a sale. When a customer wants to buy a new pair of Brooks Brothers slacks

IMPACT PRICING

they have two choices: go to the store and buy a pair now or wait until the next sale. Somebody who is not price sensitive will simply go when the need arises and pay full price. The price-sensitive customer will wait.

Almost every retail outlet has sales, some more frequently than others. Sales are a means to reach the more price-sensitive customers while still capturing some sales at full price.

In the B2B world, savvy buyers have learned to wait until the end of a vendor's quarter to get the best price. Although this isn't an explicit sale, for many companies it is so common that it may as well be advertised as the end-of-quarter clearance sale. This behavior by vendors acts as a price segmentation mechanism allowing the patient, price-sensitive buyers to get a better deal.

End-Aisle Displays (Thoroughness)

At the grocery store on the end of each aisle is a large display of a product, like Lay's Potato Chips. There is usually a relatively large sign advertising the price, possibly an indicator that this is a good price. Do customers walk down the aisle to see how much the Ruffles are? Some do and some don't.

The end-aisle display is wonderful because it implies a promotion, but the price is not necessarily a good discount. Who will see this? This same type of purchase decision happens frequently in industries other than grocery stores. A shopper sees an advertisement for a garden shed with a list price of $300 on sale for $199. It's a great deal, he buys it. Did he shop around for a better price first? Price-sensitive customers shop around. It may pay to have your product or service offered all by itself at times so the customers who aren't going to shop around don't notice if there is a better-priced product available.

Customer Behaviors: Jump This Hurdle

Purchase Ahead (Foresight)

Ski resorts in Lake Tahoe offer discount lift tickets at grocery stores in the Bay Area (a three- to four-hour drive away) to attract skiers. Price-sensitive skiers exert the effort to plan ahead and buy their lift tickets before driving up the mountain. Less price-sensitive skiers drive up the mountain without tickets and buy at full price at the ski resort. Airlines do this, as well. Tickets are much less expensive if you purchase at least 14 days prior to your flight. In this mechanism only price-sensitive customers who think ahead are able to capture the lower prices.

Loyalty Clubs (Investment)

For $25 you can become a member at Barnes and Noble. This buys you discounts on books and free shipping on your online book purchases. Who would buy this? Only loyal Barnes and Noble customers who are price sensitive would join. Customers who are not price sensitive don't want the hassle of finding their card to use it. They don't worry about the small discount they might get. Price-sensitive customers are willing to pull out their membership card. Barnes and Noble prefers their price-sensitive customers join and use the discount card because it makes them even more loyal. These price-sensitive customers get a discount at Barnes and Noble that they don't get at Amazon.com or any other bookstore. Paying $25 is a pretty big hurdle to get future discounts. Only price-sensitive, loyal customers will jump at it.

Channel/Internet

The Internet has created many new business models, several of which help segment customers by willingness to pay. Priceline is one website where you can purchase travel services by making an offer, but not knowing who the final service provider will be. Hotwire is similar, but they tell you the price without telling you the service provider. In both cases you have to make your purchase decision before they tell you the supplier. This does two things. First, it protects the published prices of the airlines and hotels. Second, more relevant to this chapter, it creates a hurdle that only price-sensitive buyers will want to jump. Customers who are willing to pay more will purchase elsewhere, and will pay more. By making the distribution channel less attractive, firms can charge less to their more price sensitive customers without losing their higher-paying customers.

Pay as You Wish

In 2007 the band Radiohead implemented a highly publicized pricing strategy for their newly released album *In Rainbow*. They made the music downloadable to anyone and everyone and asked people to pay what they thought it was worth to them. Sixty percent of the people who downloaded the album paid nothing, but 40 percent did pay. Radiohead considered this a big success. Obviously customers didn't pay how much they truly valued the album, but Radiohead received more small payments than if they had sold the album for its "fair" price and the total income far exceeded their expectations.

As other examples, public radio uses a pay-as-you-wish pricing method when they have their membership drives. Some podcasters ask for donations to keep themselves afloat. Many "freeware" authors ask for donations if you like their software. For this to work for you, your product must have a very low marginal cost (like a digital download). A more thorough description of pay-as-you-wish is available in *Smart Pricing* (see the Bibliography). The beauty of this mechanism is that you simply ask your customers to pay what they think it is worth. Those who are willing to pay more, do.

Customer Behaviors: Jump This Hurdle

Summary

Price segmentation is getting customers who differ in their willingness to pay to pay different amounts. All of the examples in this chapter achieve this by creating some hurdle that price-sensitive customers are willing to jump, but less price-sensitive customers are not.

Think through each of the examples and see if you can modify it so your company can take advantage of it.

Have you ever gone to a store and asked for a discount? It's hard to do. It makes me uncomfortable when I do it, even if I tell myself I'm doing it in the "name of science." Seriously, it is so hard to ask for a discount. Only people who are really price sensitive would ever do it. I don't know of any company who has an explicit policy of giving discounts to people who ask, but it would certainly fit this method of price segmentation. Can you think of any other behaviors that only price-sensitive people would do for a discount?

Summary Questions

✔ How can you apply each one of these in your industry?
- Coupons
- Rebates
- Sales events
- Lonely prices
- Purchase ahead
- Loyalty clubs
- Channel
- Pay-as-you-wish

✔ Can you think of any other hurdles that you can use in your industry?

Actions: What are you going to do?

IMPACT PRICING

Chapter 10

Transaction Characteristics:
At Point of Purchase

I found the greater the volume, the cheaper I could buy and the better value I could give customers.

—Frank W. Woolworth

Key Concepts

✔ Many characteristics of the transaction observable at the time of purchase are correlated with willingness to pay.

✔ Nimble pricing processes are needed to take advantage of these.

Our goal with price segmentation is to identify who's willing to pay more and who is not willing to pay as much. Oftentimes details about the transaction underway indicate price sensitivity. The most common and obvious of these is volume discounting. Customers who buy more tend to be more price sensitive. However, there are several other characteristics of transactions that can potentially identify willingness to pay. Let's look at several of these.

IMPACT PRICING

Volume

Discounts for volume purchases are plentiful. Why? One answer to this question is because it costs less to deliver. You only have to process one order. Your sales expenses are lower per part. Your marketing expenses per part are lower. It simply costs less per unit when one customer buys more than one part. Why shouldn't you pass that savings on to your customers? This answer is common, it's logical, and it's wrong.

At least it's wrong from the perspective of optimal pricing. Why should we charge less simply because it costs us less? This sounds a lot like cost-based pricing. Optimal pricing is about capturing our customers' willingness to pay for a product. The answer should be based on how customers perceive our value, not based on our costs. You may want to review the chapter on costs if you're not sure about this yet.

There are three good reasons for giving a volume-based discount, all of them based on *value.*

Customers who buy higher volumes typically spend more money. The more someone spends on something, the more effort they're willing to put into get a better price. Customers who put in more effort to find or negotiate a lower price by definition are more price sensitive. If giving them a lower price keeps them from looking to your competitors for a lower price, then you win.

For whatever reason, your competitors may charge less for higher volumes. Your customers are now comparing the price of 100 of your products vs. 100 of your competitor's, so your volume prices must be comparable (value adjusted, of course) to the volume prices of our competitors. If your competitors use volume-based pricing, you probably have to do the same just to remain competitive. Remember, your customers measure value by comparing your products and price to your competitor's products and price.

Transaction Characteristics: At Point of Purchase

For many products, especially consumer goods, the second unit is less valuable to your customer than the first. Imagine that you want to buy a CD, so you go into a music-store and shop around. You find one you really want and are ready to check out when you see a sign, "Buy one get the second one for half price." You weren't going to buy a second CD, at least not at full price, but now you might shop around and find a second one so you can take advantage of the discount. This is an example of how your willingness to pay for the second CD was less than for the first CD. Volume discounts can allow you to capture incremental sales without having to discount the first sale.

In each of these explanations, the customer who buys a higher quantity is more price sensitive than a customer who buys fewer. Hence, volume discounts are a legitimate and effective way to segment customers based on willingness to pay.

Weather

In 2005 Coca-Cola brilliantly created a unique price segmentation method and then completely botched its implementation. Coke created vending machines that knew the outside temperature so that on hot days, a cold soft drink costs more than on cold days. Certainly people value an ice-cold refreshing beverage more on hot days, so this should work great.

Here's how they messed up the execution. There were articles written about Coke's "plan to charge more for a Coke on a hot day." That was the problem. They charged more for a Coke on a hot day. People thought they were being gouged. How dare Coke take advantage of the heat to extract more money from them.

What Coke should have done is charge less for a soda on a cold day. Functionally and practically, this is the same thing as charging more on a hot day. The *big* difference is the perception of the customer. If Coke is offering a discount to motivate purchases on a cold day, that's a great thing. Even though the execution was less than stellar, the concept is still valid.

The San Francisco Giants charge less for a baseball ticket on rainy days. Same concept, better positioning. There is even a website called Blueskylocal.com to help companies invigorate business on slow days by offering discounts when the weather is bad.

Time of Day

Almost every movie theater offers matinee pricing for late morning and early afternoon shows. Obviously, customers value evening shows the most, so by charging different prices based on time of day it allows the price-sensitive buyers to spend their money at the theater without giving a discount to those who are willing to pay more.

Location

Twenty years ago, outlet malls were a rarity. To get to one, you typically had to drive a long way, fight enormous crowds, and put up with unattractive merchandise. Only people who were very price sensitive would go to an outlet mall. What a great way to segment the market based on willingness to pay. Today it seems there is an outlet mall every 50 miles and the quality of the merchandise has improved, so the hurdle to shop there is much lower.

First-Time Buyer

In the commercial garbage collection business, competitors have to be very aggressive with price to win a new customer. However, once that customer has been won, prices slowly creep up. Average customers will stick with the same waste collector for 10 years, and by the time 10 years have passed, they're often paying two to three times what they would pay if they took their business out for bid again.

Transaction Characteristics: At Point of Purchase

Satellite TV and cable companies often offer high discounts for first-time buyers. In this case it is also a needed incentive to overcome the hassle of switching providers. There are many instances where customers are price sensitive when making a first purchase decision and less price sensitive as inertia keeps them going.

Number of Quotes

In B2B, you may be able to watch the customer transactions in almost real time. One behavior that very price-sensitive companies exhibit is to request quotes from multiple channel partners. So, when a manufacturer sees the same end customer quote through several distributors, this is a demonstration that the customer is willing to expend time and energy finding a better price. This is a price-sensitive customer.

Summary

Characteristics of the transaction, or at least at the time of the transaction, can be strongly correlated with your customers' willingness to pay. Your goal is to determine what characteristics you can determine at the time of purchase to help you set prices. Many companies have some type of volume-based pricing. Can you think of any others that apply to your company?

So far we've looked at three pricing segmentation schemes: customer characteristics, customer behaviors, and transaction characteristics. Each of these describe ways to get customers to pay different prices for essentially the same product or service. Another powerful and common method of price discrimination is to create different products for segments with differing willingness to pay. This is called versioning. The concept of versioning would fit well in this part, but it fit even better in Part Three on Portfolio Pricing.

IMPACT PRICING

Summary Questions

✔ How can you apply each one of these in your industry?
- Volume
- Weather
- Time of day
- Location
- First-time buyer
- Number of quotes

✔ Can you think of other transaction characteristics that may help you determine your customers' willingness to pay?

Actions: What are you going to do?

Loyalty and Price Segmentation:
Treat Your Best Customers the Best

Do what you do so well that they will want to see it again and bring their friends.

—Walt Disney

Key Concepts

- ✔ Loyal customers have a high willingness to pay. Don't take advantage of this.
- ✔ The lifetime cost of losing a loyal customer is very high.

Price segmentation can be exceptionally valuable to your company. However, capturing value on each individual transaction is not your only consideration. Capturing value in the long term is a much better concern.

Loyal customers are hard to create and cultivate, but they are by far your most valuable customers. One characteristic about loyal customers, though, is they are willing to pay more for your product, because they are loyal. In our paradigm of price segmentation, we look for ways to charge

IMPACT PRICING

more to people who are willing to pay more. Hence if you strictly follow the price segmentation guidelines in this section you would charge loyal customers more. Don't do it.

If your loyal customers find out that you've been charging them more, they may become upset and switch loyalties. You can lose a valuable customer. As a general rule, it's best to cultivate loyal customers, keeping them happy, possibly offering them lower prices than normal. Local retailers often do this with a "Buy 10 get 1 free" card. This is the same as offering a discount to their most loyal customers. Airlines offer frequent flyer miles. Hotels offer frequent stay rewards. Many companies reward loyalty. Should you?

Previously we talked about the garbage collection service where relationships last 10 years. Prices creep up during that time so the customer is paying two to three times what a new contract customer would pay. This example is less about loyalty and more about inertia. Loyalty is when a customer regularly makes a purchase decision, and that decision is for your product. Inertia is when the customer just does what he did last time so he doesn't have to make a new decision. Cell phone service providers, satellite TV companies, and even banks have inertia. They can get away with charging existing customers more than new customers.

Most industries do not have this type of inertia. In most markets, customers make new purchase decisions every time. If you can identify your loyal customers, the ones who always choose your product, reward them—don't punish them.

Your loyal customers are your best customers. Even though they are willing to pay more, they are expensive to lose. Be cautious how you treat your truly loyal customers. Giving them your best price may very well be your best long-term profit maximizing strategy.

Loyalty and Price Segmentation: Treat Your Best Customers the Best

Summary Questions

✔ Can you identify your loyal customers?
✔ How do you reward them for their loyalty?

Actions: What are you going to do?

Part Three

Portfolio Pricing:
No Product Is an Island

This is a situation where one and one will equal three.
—*Blake Irving, Yahoo!*

Chapter 12

Versioning:
Develop the Right Product Line

Luxury goods are the only area in which it is possible to make luxury margins.

—Bernard Arnault, CEO of LVMH

Key Concepts

✔ Versioning is creating multiple versions of your product. It is common and extremely profitable.

✔ The higher up the product line, the higher the gross margin percentage.

✔ In Good, Better, Best offerings, customers who are uncertain buy Better.

So far in this text we've assumed that you have a single product and you need to put a price on it. We've seen how you can segment your market into customers who are willing to pay more and willing to pay less, and charge these customers different prices for essentially the same product. In this part we explore what happens when you have a product line, when you have more than one product, and your products are somehow related.

IMPACT PRICING

Products can be related as either substitutes or complements. When products are substitutes, it means that if a customer buys one of them, it is less likely that they will buy the other. For example, if you buy a coach seat on a flight, you are not going to also purchase a first-class seat. With substitute products you are influencing the customer's choice within your own product line to capture the most value. As you will see later in this chapter, this can be price segmentation using product characteristics.

Complementary products are ones where, when you purchase one product, you are more likely to purchase the other. One example is a hamburger and fries at McDonald's. If McDonald's can convince you to purchase a hamburger from them (instead of Burger King), then you are more likely to purchase fries from them, as well. We frequently price one complementary product to attract customers and then another product to make profit. Pricing complementary products is covered in the next chapter.

Versioning

To this point we've focused on your customers making a decision between your product and your competitor's. What if we can get them to make a choice between one of your products and another one of your products? When you offer more than one product, the situation gets more complex. The customer is deciding between your offerings, as well as between you and your competition. Although the customer's decision making is more complex, the opportunities for price to capture value become much richer.

The term *versioning* is used to describe the act of creating different versions of your product. We see versioning everywhere we look. Walk into Best Buy and see all the versions of Samsung TVs on the wall. Go to the grocery store and see all the versions of Dreyer's ice cream. Books are hardback, paperpack, audio, and e-books. Movies are released at the

Versioning: Develop the Right Product Line

theater, on DVD, on Netflix, on HBO, on network TV. The most common usage of versioning is to capture differing amounts of value from your customers. Your profits are almost guaranteed to go up by implementing versioning correctly.

Recall that price segmentation is about finding segments of customers who are willing to pay different amounts for the same or similar product and then charging them different prices. Versioning is price segmentation using product characteristics. Our objective is to identify customers who value our products differently and create product offerings that more closely capture that value.

Price segmentation in the previous section meant selling the exact same product to different people at different prices. For example, two people sitting in coach class on a flight have purchased essentially the same service and experience, but usually pay different prices. Another example is students paying less to get into the movies.

However, versioning is also a common method of price segmentation, even if the companies don't realize they're using this clever pricing mechanism. Versioning is all around us and is sometimes hard to recognize as what it is—price segmentation through product differentiation.

I went through the Burger King drive-through the other day and ordered a Whopper for $2.39. They asked if I'd like cheese, and of course I said yes. My Whopper with cheese was $2.69. The Whopper with cheese was 30 cents more! For a slice of *cheese*?

So how is this price segmentation? People who are price sensitive would never pay 30 cents for a slice of cheese. But people who aren't so price sensitive would. This is versioning. As the name implies, you create different versions of a product for customers with different levels of price sensitivity. In the Burger King case they had two versions, a Whopper with cheese and one without.

IMPACT PRICING

To execute versioning well, you need to understand your customers. You are creating choices within your product line, and you have a lot of control over the product features and prices of those choices. Knowing how your customers value the features is a great asset.

Good, Better, Better ...

The most common form of versioning is creating a product line with more features the higher you go up the line. In this type of price segmentation, most people can easily rank one product above another. For example, the Whopper is good, the Whopper with cheese is better. Coach seats on an airline are good, first-class seats are better.

The Basics

Start by defining a "bare-bones" offering. What is the least featured product you could offer that would still be functional to your customers? Think Whopper without cheese, a coach seat on an airline, a new car without an options package. In the absence of other reasons, you will price this product near the lowest gross margin you're willing to accept. The objective with this product is to capture as many price-sensitive customers as possible. These customers weren't going to pay a lot for your product anyway, but they're still profitable, and you want to service them. If not, raise prices to the point where you do want to service them.

Then add a feature or two that most people would like and price the new product higher than the bare-bones version. In terms of gross margin, the margin percentage on just the new feature should be significantly higher than the margin percentage on the bare-bones offering. Thus, the overall margin percentage on this "better" offering is higher than on the "good."

Let's look at our two examples. Burger King makes about 50 percent gross margin on a Whopper, so it's profitable and

Versioning: Develop the Right Product Line

they're happy selling it. However, they're making over 90 percent margin on that slice of cheese. The overall gross margin on a Whopper with cheese then is around 55 percent. Most people want the cheese, but price-sensitive customers won't purchase it.

The airline example is even more exaggerated. I recently looked up the price of a flight from San Francisco to LaGuardia in New York. The coach seat was $310. The first-class seat was $3,000. *Wow*! A first-class seat has about twice the room as a coach seat, so if they were charging for the space then the airline should be charging $620. So the other $2,380 is for the upgraded meal. What a meal! That's price segmentation. Anybody wealthy enough to afford the first-class ticket would probably purchase it just to be more comfortable for the five-hour flight, but anyone who is price sensitive definitely would not.

Versioning is not new. Jules Dupuit, a 19th-century economist, wrote about the railway travel business in 1849. "It is not because of the few thousand francs which have to be spent to put a roof over the third-class carriages or to upholster the third-class seats that some company or other has open carriages with wooden benches. What the company is trying to do is to prevent the passengers who pay the second class fare from traveling third class; it hits the poor, not because it wants to hurt them, but to frighten the rich." Did you catch that? Third class rail travel was hard benches *without a roof*. And they didn't do this because they couldn't afford the enhancements. They did this so anyone who could afford to travel with a roof surely would pay for it. I sure hope the airlines are not trying to think of any more ways to make coach travel less comfortable.

More Than Two

You can offer many levels of your product. The 1849 rail travel example was for third class, meaning there was also

IMPACT PRICING

second class and first class. Very long flights often offer coach, business class, and first class. Many airlines today are offering a little more room in the front of coach for an additional fee. You can create as many levels of your product as practical and allow your customers to decide how much they want to pay. One quick caution: when there are too many choices, many consumers put off the decision because it's too difficult. Don't go overboard with this.

Take Something Away

We typically think of versioning as adding features to a bare-bones offering to make a better product. However, versions can arise from explicitly taking value out. One common versioning technique in grocery stores is using generic or store brands. These products are often identical to the brand-name products, only without the brand name. Price-sensitive consumers are willing to buy the generics, while consumers with higher willingness to pay continue to buy the branded versions.

> We are clearly benefiting from the results of our segmentation strategy.
> —Paul Otellini

#impactpricing

One of my favorite examples of explicitly taking features out occurred in the early 1990s. Intel released its 80486 processor product line with two major versions, one with a math coprocessor and one without a math coprocessor. What is fascinating about this example is that they built every chip exactly the same. Every chip came off the manufacturing line as the version with the math coprocessor. Then Intel intentionally added a manufacturing step to disable the math coprocessor on its lower-end product. From a cost perspective, it cost more to build the single-core processor than the dual-core, yet they charged more for the dual-core. This is an example of Intel looking not at costs, but at

Versioning: Develop the Right Product Line

what their customers were willing to pay for, and creating the right offerings.

Finding Versions

Sometimes you don't design different versions, but the versions exist anyway. It's your job to find them. In the semiconductor industry companies frequently test to determine which parts coming off the manufacturing line have which attributes. For example, many types of semiconductors are more expensive the faster they operate. However, the semiconductor manufacturers typically don't design different speeds of their products. The manufacturing process has enough variance that each unit coming off the line has slightly different performance characteristics. The manufacturers test each part for speed and place it in the appropriate bin. Customers are willing to pay more for faster units.

Many times we can't control all the factors that create value, but we can recognize them and price appropriately. Another of my favorite examples is the San Francisco Giants. We mentioned previously they charge different prices based on weather, but they also charge different prices based on the day of the week, which team they are playing, and even who the starting pitchers are expected to be. They are simply recognizing and charging for how much their fans value different types of games.

I suspect within the next 10 years we will see differentiated pricing at the movie theaters. A movie complex with 20 screens should charge more for the latest released #1 movie with lines out the door than for a movie that has been out for several weeks. Movie theaters have begun charging more for 3D showings, so it's only a matter of time.

Special Comment on Negotiations

In the B2B world, versioning plays a vital role during negotiations. A general rule of negotiating is you don't give something without getting something in return. Every purchasing agent asks for a lower price. The most powerful response to that request is, "we can't offer you that price on this product, but we have another (lower-featured) version where we can meet that price." The book *Pricing with Confidence* by Reed and Burton describes this phenomenon in more detail.

Don't Forget to Price Right

You may already offer multiple versions. Now the question is: Are you pricing correctly? This is an easy mistake to make. The higher up in the product category you go, the higher your gross margin percentage should be.

A high-end bike store in the Midwest only builds custom bicycles. They have a formula for how to price the frame, the parts, and the labor. Every bike uses the same formula. Let's say their formula is 25 percent markup on frames and 40 percent markup on components that go onto the bike. This is "fair" in their minds. They described a customer who walked into their shop one day and ordered top-of-the-line everything. They could not build a more expensive bike. The customer didn't ask about price until the end. Obviously this was not a price-sensitive customer, and yet they used the same formula as their lowest-end bikes. To them, this was fair. How could this bike shop earn more money from these types of customers and still be "fair"? What about price segmentation on their versions? They currently use the same markup regardless of the quality of the bike or component.

What if they changed their formula (i.e., markup) so that the higher-end parts have a higher markup? They aren't singling out customers, just redefining their rules. Remember every transaction is voluntary. If they charge too much the customer will not buy. As long as they charge less than the customer's willingness to pay, they will earn the business. My rough calculations indicated this small pricing change

Versioning: Develop the Right Product Line

could put an additional $5,000 per year of profit in their pockets. That's a lot for a small bike shop owner.

The section on customer segmentation emphasized that as a general rule, price segmentation works by charging the majority of the customers a standard price and then giving a discount to people who can somehow prove they are price sensitive. (Think students at the movie theater.) Versioning is an exception. When we use versioning, we develop a lowest-cost base model and price this model at margins that are as low as we can tolerate to capture our most price-sensitive customers. Then we offer more-featured versions of the product at higher prices and higher margins to profit from our less price-sensitive customers. Don't forget to capture this extra margin.

Good, Better, Best

Good, Better, Best is an extension of versioning that takes advantage of your customers' psychological make-up.

Given the options of Good, Better, and Best, people who are unsure of what they want buy Better.

Go back and read that sentence again. It is the crux of the Good, Better, Best tactic.

Customers avoid "Best" because they're afraid of paying too much. They're even more afraid of "Good" because they are afraid to purchase a product that might not meet their needs. When uncertain, they buy "Better." Sears is famous for using this pricing tactic.

Although this might seem funny or strange, there's rational support for this behavior. Uncertain customers use the options that the sellers make available to them as information to help them make their decision. Without knowing anything else, they can infer that the company selling these products selected them for a reason. The company probably selected the "Good" option for very price-sensitive customers,

IMPACT PRICING

> **Personal Story**
>
> I've been thinking about buying the Apple iPad 2 that was recently released. They are selling the 16 GB version for only $499, the 32 GB version for $599, and the 64 GB version for $699. How can I possibly make this decision? I have no idea how much memory I'll need. If I were struggling to be able to afford one I'd certainly buy the 16 GB version. And if I were wealthy enough that $100 didn't really matter I'd purchase the 64 GB version. Since I'm neither of those and don't know what to do, I'll probably purchase the 32 GB version. What would you do? Why?

#impactpricing

and the "Best" option for the rich. Most of us are neither of these, so we buy the "Better" option *when we are uncertain*.

This tactic only works for your uncertain customers. Customers who know exactly what they need will buy exactly that, regardless of the choices. However, very few customers know with certainty exactly what they need and what is available. This tactics works in many industries.

If you currently have two versions of your offering, you should seriously consider adding a third with *more* features at a *higher* price (and feature level). This action will likely sway any of your customers who were debating between buying your "Good" and "Better" to choose "Better." You'll also likely sell some "Best" at presumably a much higher profit than your other offerings. Simply adding a "Best" option can put more profit dollars in your pocket, even if nobody buys it.

Version by Market

A less common but equally effective method of versioning is to create specific products targeted at different markets. In this situation, one product offering may not have more features than another; rather, they may have a different set of best features.

Versioning: Develop the Right Product Line

A software company created a technology to make encryption, storage, and communication seamless. They identified three specific markets for their technology: lawyers, accountants, and consultants. Each of these markets valued different features and were willing to pay different amounts. Lawyers valued secure communication and being able to share documents under attorney-client privilege. Accountants cared about storing private records. Consultants cared about secure collaboration. From a willingness-to-pay perspective, the lawyers were willing to pay the most and the consultants the least. This company was able to create a specific offering with a unique set of features for each of these markets. Most importantly, they were able to price these offerings based on their customers' willingness to pay.

Another example you may be more familiar with. The airlines have specifically broken their market into business travelers and leisure or vacation travelers. Business travelers are willing to pay much more. The airlines are able to make up features that clearly delineate these two markets. The most obvious was their requirement for a Saturday night stay in order to get the leisure traveler rate. They created two versions of their product, each targeted at a specific customer.

Summary

Versioning is an amazingly effective technique for increasing your profit. You're influencing your customer's choice within your product line. However, you can never forget how your customers perceive value. They're not only comparing products within your product line, they're also comparing them to your competition. So every version of a product you create still must be valuable to your customer relative to your competition.

The most common form of versioning is good, better, better, where each successive version is considered better than the previous one. As you go up in quality/features/ value, you should go up faster in price. Your gross margin percentage should be getting higher as you go up in the product line.

If you currently have two versions of your product, you're almost guaranteed to make more money by offering a third, more expensive version. Adding Best to Good and Better will almost certainly drive a higher percentage of customers to buy Better. Be careful about the number of versions, though. Too many and your customers will have a hard time making decisions, which means they won't.

Look around as you shop. Almost everything you want to buy has versions. The question is are these companies pricing them most profitably? Are you?

Summary Questions

- ✔ What products do you have that are substitutes?
- ✔ Are you charging a higher gross margin percentage on the more expensive ones?
- ✔ Can you add a Best offering to influence customer choice?
- ✔ Do you have different markets that need different versions?

Actions: What are you going to do?

Chapter 13

Complementary Products:
Linking and Leveraging

A good film is when the price of the dinner, the theatre admission, and the babysitter were worth it.

—Alfred Hitchcock

Key Concepts

- ✔ Know what products and features your customers use to make their choice decisions. Charge less for them.
- ✔ Know what products and features your customers don't shop for good prices and charge more for them.

When you offer products that are complements, you may have an opportunity to increase profits. Complements are when you sell one product, you increase the chance of selling a different, complementary product. The key, as it is in all of pricing, is knowing how your customers make their purchase decisions. Then you can figure out how best to make a profit.

IMPACT PRICING

Customers don't know everything. They are not omniscient and can't think of everything when making decisions. Instead, they use limited information. Your objective is to know what information they use for these choices and to be as competitive as possible in these areas so they decide in your favor. The advantage of having complementary products is you can be extremely competitive with some products and still make a reasonable profit by selling additional items to the same customers.

Loss Leader

Retail outlets sometimes use a loss leader. The classic example is milk. Grocery stores advertise the price of milk in their weekly flyers. Sometimes they advertise a price that is lower than their cost. They sell it at a loss. Of course they're doing this to get customers to come into the store. Then they will very likely sell many more items to each shopper to make up for any loss on the milk. (Have you noticed that milk is always at the back of the store so the shopper has to walk past hundreds of items?)

Grocery stores determined that people choose which store to shop at least partly by the price of milk in the weekly advertisement. By offering a low price on milk, they influence that choice. The choice decision that customers make, the one that's important for the store to influence in its favor, is where the customer chooses to shop. Once the grocery wins that choice, the customer will buy plenty of higher-margin items and the store makes money.

The item that our customer uses to make his or her choice is the "decision item." In the above example, milk is the decision item. Customers use the price of milk to help determine where to shop. "Add-on items" are the additional purchases that happen after the initial decision has been made. These are the items where you have the opportunity and should plan

Complementary Products: Linking and Leveraging

to make money. In the above example, everything else in the store is an add-on item.

Here is another example. McDonald's advertised its double cheeseburger for 99 cents. Many franchisees complained that this was below their costs and couldn't support this price, but they did it anyway. Why? Obviously, the double cheeseburger was the decision item, and fries and soft drinks are the add-ons. The franchisees receive well over a dollar for a soft drink that costs them about 15 cents to make. They can make money selling fries and soft drinks even if every customer who walks through the door buys a double cheeseburger.

The concept behind pricing complementary products is to price aggressively for decision items and price to capture value and make profit on the add-on items. Let's look at several more examples.

Durables and Consumables

A classic example is razors and blades. Gillette pioneered the concept of giving away razors so they could sell the blades that go in them. And they are still doing it. Even recently I received a new Gillette razor in the mail. In this case the razors are the decision item, and if it is free, it's very easy to make that decision. The blades are the add-ons, where the company makes its profits. The "razors and blades" pricing strategy relies on getting a durable good into the customer's possession and selling consumables after the fact.

A more modern yet extremely common example of this strategy today is printers and ink. Printers are very inexpensive relative to their cost to manufacture, but ink is expensive. Ink is such a profitable business that printer manufacturers install intelligence (with intellectual property protection) in the ink cartridges as extra incentive to buy ink from them. If you have an HP printer and you put in real HP

IMPACT PRICING

ink cartridges, then your printer will tell your computer how much ink you have left. If you use third-party ink, you don't get that feature.

Although video games (the software) aren't technically consumable, once a gamer has played the game they are likely to put it aside and buy a new one. In this respect, video game consoles and their games (software) follow the durables and consumables model as well. The Sony Playstation 3 and Microsoft Xbox 360 were sold at aggressively low margins, but Sony and Microsoft both make large royalties off of the games that play in their consoles.

If you have a durable and consumable situation, consider aggressively pricing your durable good (the decision item) with the expectation of making money on the consumables (the add-ons).

Accessories

Accessories almost always have significantly higher margins than the main item. It's common for retailers to accept relatively small margins for the decision items and much larger margins for the add-ons, or in this case, the accessories.

For example, in the bicycle world, the bicycle frame typically has a pretty small margin, the components a slightly higher margin, and post-purchase accessories like shorts and jerseys, the highest margins.

Best Buy makes about a 15 percent margin on a large flat panel TV. They make about 50 percent margin on the cables to hook that TV to your DVD player. A director at eBay described how many of their online stores will sell a large flat panel TV at cost (almost a loss leader) in the hopes of selling the accessories at a profit.

Captive Customers

One of my favorite pricing problems is "Why does popcorn cost so much at the movie theater?" There are several reasonable

Complementary Products: Linking and Leveraging

answers to that question. One of them is complementary products. Consumers choose which theater to go to based on information about the movie, the location, and maybe the price at that theater. The decision item is the movie. Most consumers do not use the price of popcorn in making this decision. Now the theater owner prices the popcorn (and all of the snacks) to maximize profits given that the customer is already in the door. Referring back to Chapter 3, this is the "Will I?" decision. Will his customers buy popcorn? Not "which popcorn will they buy?" He knows that if a moviegoer buys popcorn, the owner gets to sell it.

Another fact you may not know, movie theaters make very little money on ticket sales. The pricing structure is set up so the producers get most (90 percent) of the ticket revenue, especially the first few weeks after release when the demand is high. A theater makes most of its money on the concessions. That doesn't explain why they price popcorn so high, but it might help you feel better about paying the exorbitant price next time you go to the movie.

What other examples of captive customers are there? Once a family pays to get into an amusement park, that is where they will buy their snacks. We already talked about the price of a soda at McDonald's. Airports charge slightly higher prices for food. They know they can charge more, but if they charge a lot more people will either eat before they arrive at the airport or will wait until after they've left.

Captive customers are simply another example of complementary products, where the customer makes a choice based on the decision item, and the company has the opportunity to make money on the add-ons.

De-Bundling

Every complementary example so far is based on knowing which products our customers use to make their decision. Let's go a level deeper and ask, Which features of a product offering does a customer use to make his decision? If you find features the customer doesn't use in the decision process, can you unbundle them and charge for them?

The best example of this right now is the airlines. Do you remember when the price of a coach seat included a meal? Airlines unbundled that. They now sell meals on the plane. Do you remember when the price of a coach seat included up to two pieces of checked luggage? The airlines unbundled that. They now charge to check a bag.

Why does this work? It's because the decision item is the transportation from one city to another. What would have happened if only one airline unbundled the luggage feature, slightly lowered the price of the flight and made up the profit on the baggage fee? When travelers compared prices of the flights they would see this airline had lower prices and would choose them. Because the decision item is the flight, not the total cost of travel.

What about the late night infomercials? They put together a deal so great nobody can refuse. They price it at *only* $19.99 (plus $6.95 shipping and handling). They pitch this so the decision item is the $19.99, but pick up extra income from S&H.

Look closely at your offering. Is there a feature or two you can de-bundle to give your decision item a more aggressive price? Remember you can make that profit back selling the de-bundled add-on feature.

Bundling

Unlike the complementary pricing techniques reviewed above, bundling is not based on charging a low price for the decision item and a higher margin for the add-ons. Instead, bundling is most commonly used to capture additional revenue from a customer who has already decided to purchase one of your products.

Complementary Products: Linking and Leveraging

Every fast food place now has a "meal deal." A local McDonald's has the following pricing:

Big Mac – $2.99

Small fries – $1.39

Small soda – $1.49

Big Mac meal deal – $5.39

Their objective is to sell each customer more. A customer walks in the door thinking they want to buy a Big Mac. They may look at the price of the bundle and instead choose to go for all of it. Or, they may walk in planning to purchase a Big Mac and a soda, but then the fries are only a little bit more.

Of course the trade-off is that McDonald's makes less money on customers who would have purchased all three anyway. They have apparently made the calculations that offering the meal deal is much more profitable.

Finding bundling opportunities is somewhat complex, but here's a way to get started. Find a couple of offerings that are relatively similar in value. These items should be weak complements, meaning that if a customer buys one, they probably like and would want the other item but don't usually buy it. Then, put the two products together into a bundle and offer them at a discount off of the price of both items.

One example might be two DVDs. *Sleepless in Seattle* may sell for $20 and *Two Weeks Notice* may also sell for $20. These are both romantic comedies. It would be fair to assume that someone walking in the door most likely would not purchase both. However, if that person was going to purchase *Sleepless in Seattle*, they would probably like *Two Weeks Notice* even though she wasn't going to purchase it. What if there was a bundle of both DVDs for only $32? The buyer purchasing *Sleepless* may decide to buy the bundle instead. As long as the cost on *Two Weeks Notice* is less than $12 the company makes more money by selling the bundle.

Product Funnel

The product funnel concept is excellent for consultants, speakers, and individual contractors. You may be familiar with a version of the sales funnel, where prospects fall into the funnel as leads, become qualified leads, move to opportunities, then become paying customers. There are fewer and fewer people closer to the bottom of the funnel. The important concept of the sales funnel is you have to put a lot of prospects in the top to get a few customers out the bottom.

The product funnel is similar, but with a twist. You'll want to create a series of products or offerings of increasing price. Your inexpensive products are at the top of the funnel and your most expensive items are at the bottom. The concept is to transition your customers though the funnel from buying your inexpensive items at the top to purchasing your more expensive items lower down. For example, you may start out giving a free speech and collecting the names and e-mail addresses for your mailing list. Many of these people may read your blog, where you make a few dollars from advertising. A few may decide to purchase your book for $20. Some move on to buy your CD set for $50. Some go to your paid workshop for $450. Some move on to hire you in one-on-one coaching or for a consulting project for several thousand dollars.

Notice how you transported customers from inexpensive interactions to higher-priced products. This only happens after you've built a suite of complementary products. One reason this product funnel works so well is that if you're a small independent business, very few people (if any) will meet you and immediately spend thousands of dollars with you. This funnel allows you to make some money while you build your brand and reputation with each individual customer.

Complementary Products: Linking and Leveraging

Summary

Complementary products have the ability to increase your profitability if you use them well. As with all pricing, you start by learning how your customers make their decisions. For complements, pay particular attention to which products and/or features they actually consider when making their choices. These are the decision items, the ones where you need to win the choice battle. Price the decision items aggressively. Any products or features that customers don't consider when making the original choice decision are the add-on items and are opportunities for making a little additional profit. Price the add-on items with higher margins. The more revenue you earn from add-on products, the more aggressively you can afford to price the decision items, in turn winning you more business. This decision item vs. add-on item structure works with loss leaders, durables and consumables, accessories, captive customers, and de-bundling. Most of the extra profit in complementary products comes from understanding and correctly pricing the decision items and the add-on items.

There are two other pricing strategies for complementary goods that are not tied directly to the decision item/add-on item structure. These are bundling and the product funnel. Bundling is a method to sell more to a customer than you likely would have without bundling. It is definitely worth experimenting with.

For any independent consultants or businesspeople, you want to clearly understand and implement the product funnel. Your customers will only spend a lot of money with you after they trust you and have built a relationship. Taking your customers through the product funnel gives you the time to build that relationship.

IMPACT PRICING

Summary Questions

- ✔ What products do you have that are complements?
- ✔ Do you *really* know what products and features your customers use to choose you over your competition? Write them out.
- ✔ What can you de-bundle and not affect your customer's choice?
- ✔ What can you bundle?
- ✔ Are you building a product funnel? Should you?

Actions: What are you going to do?

Chapter 14

Free:
How to Get Paid for Free

So charging a price, any price, creates a mental barrier that most people won't bother crossing.

—Chris Anderson

Key Concepts

✔ Free is a million times better than any price.

✔ Offer real value for free to help sell products for money.

One of the most insightful and thought-provoking books on "pricing" I've read recently is one by Chris Anderson, *Free*. I include a discussion of "free" here because it's a powerful concept that every company should consider. Free only works when it's part of a product portfolio. You need something to sell. If your only product is free, then you make no money.

The basic premise of free from a supply and demand point of view is:

IMPACT PRICING

- **Supply.** Costs are going down dramatically. The marginal cost of delivering information is close to zero.
- **Demand.** Consumers behave in a radically different way for a free product than even for one with a very small price.

In this book we focus only on the demand side of free. People behave as though free is a million times better than any price. In a purely mathematical sense, free is infinitely better.

Free has many different meanings. Buy-one-get-one-free is very different from a free sample. A free sample is *genuinely free*, while buy-one-get-one-free is really only a 50 percent off offer—but you must take two of the item. Genuinely free is just that—something you can get without having to open your wallet. But, more important, it's something you get without having to give anything (time, energy, or attention) in exchange.

Free is possibly the most powerful word used in marketing, but it is used in so many different contexts. There are free trials, free TV and radio if you watch the commercials, free "lite" versions of software, free blogs, free e-mail, and many more. Not all of these are genuinely Free. If we want the windfall of free, we need to offer products as close as possible to genuinely free. Here are several examples of genuinely free offerings.

Free samples. We talked about the razors and blades scenario, where the razors and a blade were given away for free. It's common for companies that make consumable products to give away free samples for trial.

Free information. Many people and companies give away free information. Instead of selling articles to magazines or writing books, they publish in blogs and provide free e-books to build a reputation for the writer. The hope is that in exchange for this free information, when the reader needs additional information or related services they know where to

Free: How to Get Paid for Free

go. Almost any company can create free yet valuable information related to their product or industry. Think of it as intelligent advertising.

Free network membership. Many businesses are more valuable to the customers when there are more users. For example, sites like LinkedIn and Facebook require millions of users to be successful. By offering a lot of value for free, they can build their network.

There are many ways to turn large networks into money. Some, like Facebook, sell advertising. Others, like LinkedIn, sell upgraded memberships to charge for additional services (see Freemiums below). Some very large networks, like Twitter, are still looking for ways to monetize its user base. There is little doubt they will succeed. They have captured users' attention, and that is worth money.

Freemiums. This is a relatively new word that means giving away a version of your product absolutely free in the hopes that a small percentage of the users will buy an upgraded version. This is common in software where many companies offer lite versions. These versions are free to use forever, but some key and valuable features are only available with paid versions. To implement a freemium, you want to create a lite version that's valuable to many—but not too valuable. In that way, people who really find the product useful will want it enough to pay for a full-featured version. For hundreds if not thousands of examples of this, go to Apple's iTunes App store and look at the apps that have both free and paid versions. The providers of these free applications are hoping you'll upgrade to their full version. Giving away the lite version costs them very little.

Another interesting example of a freemium is *The Wall Street Journal*. You can read some of its content online, but not all. To have access to it all, you must pay for a subscription. LinkedIn also works on a freemium model. It is free to

IMPACT PRICING

join and use. However, there are features like Inmail and advanced search that you can access only if you upgrade to a paying membership.

Industry experts say that the conversion rate from free to the paid version ranges from 0.05 to 5 percent with an average conversion rate of 2 percent.

The idea is to build an application and get it in the market where a lot of people want it, as long as it's free. You're building buzz. You're creating word-of-mouth advertising. Then you need to add enough value that people are willing to upgrade. If you can build a business model where you can afford to have 99 percent of your customers use your product free, then freemium may be the way to go.

Freemiums are both a complement and a substitute. It's a complement in that the more adoptions you get for the lite product, the larger the base of people who may be willing to purchase the upgraded version. Many people try the free version first and then upgrade. However, it's a substitute because many people use the free version and never upgrade. The freemium may be good enough.

Ad supported. Advertising-based business models are pretty close to free. The customer receives entertainment or information on TV and in exchange is exposed to advertising. Most of Google's business is free in this sense. Free Internet search, free Gmail, free Google Docs. The only thing Google asks for in return is some screen space where it can advertise. We don't even have to click on the ads. Network TV and radio are other examples of ad-supported free.

Free trials. Free is sometimes deceiving, yet consumers are savvy and quickly see through these tricks. Free 30-day trials of software seem free, but they really aren't. The user must invest the time and energy to become proficient at a software package that will be taken away in 30 days if they don't buy. Consumers have learned that their time is important, and investing time is like investing money. A 30-day trial requires an investment in time. This is different from a freemium which is *genuinely free*.

If you build a physical product, what can you give away for free? The most cost-effective items for any company to give away are digital, something your customers can download over their computers. This scales, and there are almost no variable costs involved. You can write a blog to share your expertise. You can create interesting podcasts or videos to share.

Remember though, you need to give away something that customers will value. This is not a sales pitch. Rather it's you, genuinely and freely sharing with your potential customers. This concept became most clear to me after watching Darren LaCroix speak. Darren talks about several things, but at the time he gave a one-hour keynote to a room full of Toastmasters. He spent 57 minutes of that hour really teaching us how to become better speakers, and he was fantastic. At the end of his talk he asked the audience, "Have I given you enough value? Have I earned the right to tell you about my products?" Of course the audience said yes. He spent only three minutes explaining what products he had for sale at the back of the room. I didn't buy any. But I did walk away in wonder at what I had just witnessed. Darren honestly packed as much free information into that 57-minute speech as he could. His attitude was "I have so much more information than just this one hour. If you liked this hour, you may want more of me in either products or future workshops."

I have since become a close follower of Darren. He gives away a ton of information, much of which I've absorbed. He also sells a lot of items, many of which I've now purchased. Darren attracted me with his free products, but he's certainly made money off of me as I go down his product funnel. That is exactly how free is supposed to work.

Summary

Free is a powerful concept. It really is a million times more effective than any price, no matter how low, you might set on your offering. In this digital age every company and businessperson can create free offerings and benefit from them. Be careful. Go into this with a truly giving attitude. What can you honestly give away for free, that has real value to your potential customers, that can eventually lead to revenue-generating sales? Certainly you have knowledge that can be valuable to others. Find a way to share it, and subtly get credit. Customers will appreciate it and knock on your door.

Summary Questions

- ✔ What are you offering for free?
- ✔ What could you offer for free?
- ✔ Who would care?

Actions: What are you going to do?

Pricing Dynamics:
Prepare for Change

Cutting prices is usually insanity if the competition can go as low as you can.

—Michael Porter

Introduction to Pricing Dynamics:
Customer Expectations

Don't manage—lead change before you have to.

—Jack Welch

Key Concepts

✔ Customers hate price increases. Avoid them.

✔ Choose between EDLP and Hi-Lo, even if you aren't a retailer.

✔ Assuming Hi-Lo, be sure to set a higher list price.

This chapter was originally titled Introduction to Dynamic Pricing, but the phrase "Dynamic Pricing" is gaining a specific meaning of its own. The popular business press now uses *dynamic pricing* to mean rapidly changing prices based on yield management and variance in demand. For example, in April 2011 there were headlines like "Ticketmaster to Implement Dynamic Pricing System."

The fundamental concepts behind this definition of dynamic pricing were covered in the sections on segmentation and versioning. This chapter focuses on changing prices, but at a slower rate than implied by the literature. Hence, I've change the title of this chapter to "Pricing Dynamics," an accurate term to describe what is really covered.

Customers Despise Price Increases

Prices change. Actually, everything around pricing changes, and that often requires price changes. Your costs change. The price of oil is volatile, so transportation costs change. Competitors enter and exit the market. Customer needs and tastes change over time. Distribution technologies change. Your own product portfolio grows. Technology continues to advance. And of course the economy goes from boom times to bust and back. Every one of these changes can motivate you to raise or lower your prices.

No matter the cause, the single rule that should drive your thinking about changing prices is this: Customers hate price increases. They like discounts, but they hate having to pay more.

Imagine you're working with a contractor to paint your house. As the job nears completion, the contractor says to you, "We didn't need as much paint as I estimated. I'll knock $100 off the bill." You feel pretty good about that. What if instead he said, "We used more paint than I estimated. I've added $100 to your bill." You would probably be ticked off. Compare the amount of pleasure from the $100 windfall to the amount of pain from the $100 price increase. If you're like most people, the level of pain exceeds the level of pleasure.

Customers dislike price increases a lot more than they like price decreases. Imagine the following scenario. You have a product at a certain price. You go to a customer and tell him that you have to raise the price by 10 percent. He's going to be upset about that. The next day you go back and tell him you can give him the product at the old price. What

Introduction to Pricing Dynamics: Customer Expectations

do you think his level of happiness is relative to before you changed any prices? Most customers would be less happy even though they get the same price again.

Run the same thought experiment in reverse. You tell the customer one day he gets a 10 percent discount, and the next day you take it back. Is he happier than before you changed the price at all? Probably not. In both of these thought experiments we find that the pain from the price increase was greater than the pleasure from the same sized price decrease. I can't say this enough. Customers really don't like price increases.

> **People Hate Price Increases**
>
> I'm a Netflix subscriber and have been for a few years. I used to subscribe to the three-DVD program with the Blu-ray option. About six months ago they raised their prices on the Blu-ray option. Although I like to think I'm rational, I spent an hour or more fuming, searching for alternatives. In the end I reduced my subscription down to one DVD per month. I wanted to punish Netflix for raising my price. I used to be a big Netflix fan, telling all of my friends about the benefits I received and how I used it. I don't do that anymore. I feel foolish sharing this story where I appear less than rational, but it drives home the point: People hate price increases. Have you ever "punished" a company for raising prices? I'd love to hear about it.

#impactpricing

The lesson in all this is obvious: try very hard to avoid raising prices.

Start High, Then Discount

If you start by pricing high and then offer discounts, you have a better chance of avoiding price increases. This strategy has many more advantages.

Skimming. For new products, skimming is the act of starting out with a high price, selling to all the customers with a

IMPACT PRICING

high willingness to pay, and then lowering the price to sell to customers with a lower willingness to pay. This is a relatively accepted pricing strategy by consumers as long as you don't lower prices too quickly. Remember the Apple iPhone story in Chapter 2. Another advantage of entering the market this way is you have a nice high price so you can offer discounts or special deals to attract customers. See the reference price section below for more on this.

Price as a signal of quality. Price is a strong indicator of quality. I just did a quick search on Buy.com and found a men's Croton watch, normally priced at $500 on sale for $79.99. My first reaction was, what a great deal. Maybe I need a new watch. This one has to be good. After a little additional searching on the Internet I found that Newegg also sells it for the same price. Then I found it at Kohl's discount department store. It's probably not that good of a watch. However, the $500 price was initially used as an indicator of quality.

This Croton watch may be an example of a company using high price to trick the consumer into thinking it's high quality. However, if you really do have a high-quality product, nobody will believe it's high quality if your price is low. Start with a high price.

Reference prices. People like discounts. They like knowing they're getting a good deal. But what does "a good deal" mean? It means they are comparing the price they have to pay with some reference price that exists in their mind. The reference price could be a list price, like the Croton watch, or it could be the last price paid, or the price paid for a competitive product. Regardless, if you start with a higher price and then offer discounts you're more likely to shift your customer's reference price upward. The higher your customer's reference price, the more likely you make him feel like he's getting a good deal so the more likely you will get the sale.

Introduction to Pricing Dynamics: Customer Expectations

Customer segmentation. We devoted five chapters to this topic, but here's a reminder. By starting with a high price we have the opportunity to capture our customers with a higher willingness to pay at a higher price. Then we have room to discount to capture those who are more price sensitive. For example, having a temporary sale captures price-sensitive customers who probably wouldn't have purchased at full price.

Escalations. In the B2B world, large customers always negotiate prices. It's common to have a price range that your sales force can offer, but your best customers seem to need prices below whatever floor you set. Companies set up procedures to escalate specific quotes to higher and higher levels of authority in the organization. For startups, the authority usually gets to the CEO rather quickly. For large corporations, the CEO rarely sees an escalation. Regardless, starting with higher prices allows you to meet your largest customers' expectations of deep discounts.

Quarter- or year-end discounts. Another common B2B behavior is the quarter-end discount. It seems that at the end of every quarter, companies are a little behind in their bookings. They need a big sales surge to make their expected numbers. To achieve this, they make special deals with their customers, saying if you buy before the end of the quarter you can have this discounted price. Many people believe this is a bad habit, that "we're simply training our customers to wait until the quarter-end." They may be right. However, another view on this is that they are segmenting their customers. Price-sensitive customers plan and buy at quarter-end while less price-sensitive customers buy throughout the quarter. In the end, you have to decide if you're truly capturing what your customers are willing to pay.

Automatic markdowns. A pricing strategy made famous by Filene's Basement in 1909 is the automatic markdown. At

IMPACT PRICING

Filene's Basement, clothes were put on the shelf at the starting price. After 12 days, there were discounted by 25 percent. The discount was increased to 50 percent six days later and to 75 percent six days after that. If the item didn't sell within six days of the 75 percent discount day, they were given to charity. This strategy worked exceptionally well, especially for items like women's dresses, where scarcity and the time-sensitive nature of fashion drove consumers to buy early. The book *Smart Pricing* (see Bibliography) has an entire chapter dedicated to this concept.

EDLP vs. Hi-Lo

Retailers choose a strategy, either EDLP or Hi-Lo. But non-retailers should understand this basic concept, as well. It drives your pricing behavior.

EDLP stands for Every Day Low Prices. In this strategy, retailers have very low prices (every day) and fewer sales events. Walmart has been famous for emphasizing EDLP. In 2007, Walmart was seen moving away from EDLP, but in 2010 their new CEO said that Walmart would restore their EDLP strategy. Consumers view EDLP stores as lower cost, so price-sensitive people are comfortable shopping in these stores.

Hi-Lo retailers are the ones who typically charge high prices and then have significant sales events. Brooks Brothers is a high-end men's clothing retailer with relatively high prices. They have a few big sales events each year. Nordstrom, Macy's, and even JC Penney all use the Hi-Lo strategy. Hi-Lo stores have the advantage that they are able to capture some revenue at full prices from nonprice-sensitive customers. They are also able to build excitement with the price-sensitive customers when they have sales events.

Introduction to Pricing Dynamics: Customer Expectations

Although this is a retail strategy, it's a great lead-in to the strategic question every company needs to answer. Are you going to price aggressively all the time to create a low-price image or are you going to price a little higher to skim some of the market while leaving room to offer discounts? Most companies implement the equivalent of the Hi-Lo strategy, setting a higher list price and then offering discounts in certain circumstances.

If you want to adopt the equivalent of the EDLP strategy, you're committing to compete on price. There are fewer opportunities to segment your customers based on willingness to pay, and you will have to focus even more of your resources to lower your costs to stay cost competitive. And then you're really at the mercy of your suppliers. If they raise their prices, your costs go up. Then you won't have any buffer room to absorb small cost increases.

If it isn't obvious, my opinion is you should probably think of yourself like a Hi-Lo company. EDLP works for some companies, but it removes a lot of the power of pricing from your arsenal.

Summary

Customers hate price increases. Don't do it.

Knowing this, what decisions can you make to avoid future price increases? The recommendation of this chapter is to set relatively high prices and then offer discounts as appropriate. This pricing strategy affords you the buffer to absorb small cost increases without having to raise your prices. At the same time this high initial price enables many other pricing strategies that rely on having the extra margin that will allow you to offer discounts. So unless you have an explicit desire to compete on price, start high, then discount.

IMPACT PRICING

Summary Questions

✔ How can pricing high and then discounting help you win customers?
✔ Are you a Hi-Lo company?
✔ Do you have a typical target margin? What is it?
✔ What is the lowest margin you accept? Is this your Hi-Lo range?

Actions: What are you going to do?

Chapter 16

Responding to the Economy:
The 800-Pound Gorilla

A lot of companies have chosen to downsize, and maybe that was the right thing for them. We chose a different path. Our belief was that if we kept putting great products in front of customers, they would continue to open their wallets.

—Steve Jobs

Key Concepts

✔ During a recession, resist price decreases. Frame discounts as temporary.

✔ When costs go up, explore all your options before raising prices.

Unfortunately, changes in the economy are going to prompt changes in your pricing. Here we take a brief look at two negative economic situations: recession and inflation. In both cases, whole books could be written on how to compete. We're going to discuss a few high-level ideas on pricing in these situations.

IMPACT PRICING

Recessions

During a recession, consumer purchase behavior changes, which drives large changes in most markets. Shoppers spend fewer dollars by either purchasing less expensive goods or reducing the number of purchases.

Your first reaction will be to lower prices. Resist this. In the end you may have to lower prices, but resist for as long as you can. First, go back to basics. Are you creating and communicating real value? Are you charging different customers different prices? Are you developing and taking advantage of a product portfolio? All of these are discussed in previous chapters. A recession exacerbates the need to get these fundamentals right.

During a recession, not all customers are cutting back. Can you find a way to segment the customers who are reducing their spending from those who aren't? One method may be to broaden the low end of your product portfolio. Make sure you have attractive choices for the customers who aren't spending as much, but not too attractive so the customers who are not cost cutting will continue to make their regular choices.

When customers stop buying in a category, the market shrinks, and that makes all competitors nervous. It's likely that your competitors will lower their prices in an attempt to maintain current levels of business. If this is the case, you have to do something. You can't let your competitors take your entire market share. If at all possible, compete using temporary discounts. Try to not lower your prices. Coupon usage goes way up during a recession. Try coupons. Try frequent sales. If you simply lower your prices, it will be difficult to increase them when a recession ends.

Subway provides an interesting example of this. Going into the recession Subway found a powerful pricing strategy, $5 footlongs. This worked because $5 is lower than one would expect to pay for a footlong sub and more importantly, 5 is such a memorable and powerful number. Subway's sales increased quickly. But now they have firmly set $5 as the price for a footlong in our minds. How will they raise prices again as we come out of the recession?

During recessions many companies seem to be looking for the magic elixir to fix their business model. There isn't one. Times are tough for everyone. Continue to focus on the fundamentals of value, customer segmentation, and portfolio pricing. Most importantly, try to frame any pricing concessions to look temporary. You will want to bring prices back up after the recession.

Inflation

> A nickel ain't worth a dime anymore.
> —Yogi Berra

#impactpricing

Luckily in the United States we haven't had to deal with high inflation rates for several years. However, the two to three percent average inflation rate adds up over time. Inflation means your costs go up. If you don't increase prices then your profit margins go down. Yet, customers hate price increases. So how can you increase prices?

First the good news: your competitors are likely thinking the exact same thing. So if one of you takes the lead, the others are likely to follow. However, hold off raising prices too quickly. You have several other options to explore first.

Cut variable costs. Is there a way to reduce costs of your offering without significantly affecting your customers' perception of your product? This is extremely common in the packaged food industry. What used to be 28 ounces of Prego spaghetti sauce is now 26 ounces. A package of Rolos used to have 11 delicious chocolate caramel chews. Now there are 10. What looks like a half-gallon (64 oz) of Breyer's ice cream

IMPACT PRICING

is now 48 ounces. Customers quickly recognize price increases, but not so quickly recognize reductions in product quantity, especially when the size of the packaging remains about the same. Do you have some costs you can lower without being blatantly obvious to your customers?

> Inflation makes balloons larger and candy bars smaller.
> —David L. Kurtz

#impactpricing

Debundle. Look for something that costs you money that you can debundle from the purchase and charge to customers who want that feature. This allows you to possibly lower prices or at least maintain prices for customers who don't use the debundled feature. At least you've only raised prices on some of your customers. Airlines have recently debundled checked luggage, which means they now charge for checking bags. This would have been more readily accepted by their customers had they announced they were simultaneously lowering the prices of their flights for people who don't check bags.

Introduce new products. It's possible to create a new but similar product with a slightly different feature set. Charge more for the new product and attempt to move as many customers as possible to the new product. If the situation allows, you may be able to discontinue the old product altogether.

Raise fees. When gas prices hit $4 per gallon, many companies added a fuel surcharge to their bill. This extra fee isn't looked at as a price increase but as passing some cost increases through. Many customers do not consider such fees when making purchase decisions. Raising fees is preferable to simply raising prices.

Raise prices. If you have no choice but to raise prices, at least blame inflation. Customers become very angry if they believe you're increasing your profit at their expense, but are more accepting if they believe you're simply passing on

Responding to the Economy: The 800-Pound Gorilla

costs. Apologize to your customers for your price increase, but explain how your costs are going up and you have no choice. Do something nice for those who stick with you, like give them a coupon for a discount to the old price for a limited time.

Summary

The economy goes up and down, which has the effect of driving your prices up and down, as well. In recessions, resist the pressure to lower prices. Try special discounts, coupons, anything. When the recession ends, you'll want to get prices back to pre-recession levels and as you've now read many times, customers hate price increases. Think ahead.

During times of inflation you face real pressure to increase prices. When your costs increase beyond a certain point, you'll need to raise your prices. However, your goal is to do it infrequently and intelligently. Explore the alternative ways you can increase the amount your customers are willing to pay before you actually "increase price."

Summary Questions

- ✔ What strategies could you have used better going into the recession?
- ✔ As we come out of the recession, what strategies will you use to increase prices?
- ✔ Are you prepared for the next recession?
- ✔ What strategies are you going to use during the coming inflation?

Actions: What are you going to do?

Chapter 17

Responding to Competitors:
Darn Them

If you don't have a competitive advantage, don't compete.
—Jack Welch

Key Concepts

✔ Strategize ahead of time how you will respond to competitor price changes.

✔ The only way to win a price war is to have the lowest costs, and even that doesn't assure victory.

What do you do when your competitors change their prices? You really have only two choices: respond or ignore them.

Value-based pricing calculations are based on the price of a competitor's product. If the competitor's price goes up or down, then these calculations indicate you should move your price up or down, as well. The actual math implied that for every $1 move your competitor makes, you need to move the same amount. Just don't move too quickly.

IMPACT PRICING

Segmentation. This is a great time to revisit customer segmentation. Does your competitor really serve the same customers as you? If so, can you segment the market so you lower prices only to customers who really consider this competitor? We see this frequently in the airline industry. When Southwest Airlines would enter a new market, offering lower prices to specific destinations, the major airlines responded with lower prices, but not across-the-board lower prices. They didn't have to lower their first-class price, nor did they have to lower their prices for business customers who typically book at the last minute because these tended to be their loyal customers used to frequent flyer perks.

Notice in this example products that are highly differentiated don't need to be discounted, nor do products that are targeted to different customer groups. If you want to be somewhat immune to competitive price pressure, focus on differentiating your products (adding value) and targeting customer segments with offerings designed for them.

Do your customers know? Often your customers don't know the prices of your competitor's products. You only need to respond if your customers know. What percentage of your customers track both your prices and your competitors' prices? If it's only a few, you may not need to respond.

Why did they do it? Another step to take before responding is to read the news. Try to find out why your competitor made a price change. They may be attempting to get rid of excess inventory, or they may be trying to fill a factory. Their costs may have gone up. In many industries, companies announce their price changes and the reasons for them in the industry press. The price change may be temporary, in which case it's probably not necessary for you to follow suit.

Responding to Competitors: Darn Them

Price Wars

> Competition whose motive is merely to compete, to drive some other fellow out, never carries very far. The competitor to be feared is one who never bothers about you at all, but goes on making his own business better all the time.
>
> —Henry Ford

#impactpricing

As a general rule, price wars are bad, and you want to avoid them.

The common cause of price wars is someone trying to increase market share. When a CEO proclaims that the company needs to gain market share, that usually means you have to take share from your competitors. The fastest way to do that is by lowering your prices. You reduce your price, and more people choose your offering over those of your competitors. Voilà, your market share goes up.

But wait, this is only true *if* your competitors do not lower their prices as well. What would you do if your competitor lowered its prices in an effort to grab market share? Probably lower yours to match their decrease. That's likely what your competitor will do in the same circumstances. They may not be aggressive, but they won't sit back and let you take their share, so they lower their prices. Now both companies have the same market share as before only at lower prices. Certainly this wasn't worth it.

Both companies have less profit and are less well off than before the price decrease. The initial aggressor may do this over and over (after all, the CEO wants to grow market share) until they finally realize they will not "win" a price war. By then, the damage is done.

Don't use price as a lever to increase market share unless you are certain you are in a position to win a price war.

IMPACT PRICING

What does it mean to win a price war? It doesn't mean putting your competitor out of business. What it should mean is ending up with more profit when the price war is over than when it started. At the end of a price war your prices are lower, so if your profits are to be higher then you can make them up in three places: (1) increased market share, (2) market growth, and (3) lower costs.

It's important for you to understand and recognize the conditions under which a price war makes sense. You'll want to know this in case you're in a position to win the war, but you absolutely must recognize the conditions where your competitor may choose to start and likely win the price war.

Increased market share. Significantly increased market share is only possible for companies that don't have large market share today. A dominant company with over 50 percent share is much less likely to start a price war than a company with 20 percent share. It's much more painful for a dominant company to initiate or respond to price decreases.

Market growth. In many new markets, lowering prices makes the market grow more quickly. The flat panel TV market is a recent example where the prices started high, and as the prices fell more and more people purchased them. If the industry demand curve is steep (small price changes significantly affect overall demand), then the industry has potential to host a price war. In these markets, driving down prices increases the number of customers, which can grow the size of the overall pie.

Lower costs. If a company can dramatically lower its costs by increasing volume, then it's more likely to start a price war. Although its price per unit is lower, so is its cost per unit. This could result in an overall gross margin that's the same or even higher than before. Even if the margin is lower than before, the lower costs can offset the needs for addi-

Responding to Competitors: Darn Them

tional sales through market share or market growth. Multiplying this new unit margin times a larger sales volume can make the company more profitable after the price war.

If one exists, the only winner of a price war is the company with the lowest costs.

Watch out for companies in China and the Asia Pacific countries. These companies start out with relatively low market share compared to their global competitors. They are known for their very low cost of manufacturing products. Most important, the industry demand curves in China tend to be much steeper than in the United States for most products. Mature markets in the U.S. are growth markets in China as their population becomes wealthier. If you manufacture a product and don't currently have aggressive Chinese competitors, watch out. You will.

For two detailed examples of successful price wars by Chinese companies, read chapter 3 of *Smart Pricing* (see Bibliography).

Surviving a price war. You don't have to win a price war; you have to survive it. To survive, simply get out of the way. This doesn't mean quit the business or leave the market. It means differentiate your products and segment your customers. If you create products that are truly differentiated, you will still be able to sell them at a premium. The overall price may be forced down by your aggressive competitor, but you can still capture some share at a price premium simply due to your uniqueness. In the American vs. Southwest story above, American Airlines didn't have to lower their prices on first-class tickets because Southwest didn't offer first-class service.

Segment your market. Know which customers are willing to pay for what you offer. American Airlines continued to charge high prices to business travelers because Southwest also didn't cater to them.

IMPACT PRICING

Summary

Value-based pricing is all about capturing what your customer is willing to pay for. What your customer are willing to pay is directly related to your competitor's prices. So as your competitor changes prices, value-based pricing indicates you should respond. However, you should only respond if you've done the absolute best you can at segmenting the market, at portfolio pricing, and at differentiating your products. Before responding, revisit all the pricing fundamentals to determine if there's something else you can do to be more effective.

When it comes to price wars, think hard. Who in your industry could start one? How could you survive it? How could you win it? Since you never know what your competitors are thinking, always remain vigilant controlling your costs.

Summary Questions

- ✔ Do you have potentially aggressive competitors with low market share?
- ✔ How are your costs compared to your competitors?
- ✔ Are you in a highly elastic market?

Actions: What are you going to do?

Chapter 18

Product Life Cycle:
Prices Change with Age

We are always saying to ourselves ... we have to innovate. We got to come up with that breakthrough. In fact, the way software works ... so long as you are using your existing software ... you don't pay us anything at all. So we're only paid for breakthroughs.

—Bill Gates

Key Concepts

✔ Markets change in predictable ways. Price strategically to take advantage of this.

✔ Pricing at product introduction is critical. Choose your strategy wisely.

Products go through relatively predictable life cycles: introduction, growth, maturity, and decline. Prices change throughout the product life cycle. These price changes are driven by the typical changes in the market throughout a product life cycle. The number of *customers* starts small, then grows, remains stable, then declines. The number of *competitors* starts small, then grows, remains stable, then declines. Manufacturing costs, if any, start high, then decrease, and become stable.

Although prices can and do respond to changes in the market, knowing the predictability of some of these market changes can help you price your offerings to stay in front of these expected changes.

Before going through pricing and the product life cycle stages, let's revisit the concepts of neutral, penetration, and skimming pricing in light of what we've learned about value-based pricing.

Consider one of your products and go through the value-based pricing process. If you choose to price at or near the price that value-based pricing suggests, you are using *neutral pricing*. The intent is to be competitive with others in the market after differentiation has been considered.

If your price is significantly below the value-based pricing suggestion, you are using *penetration pricing*. The intent here is to undercut your competition and grow market share. If you price significantly above the value-based pricing suggestion, you are *skimming* with the intention of capturing more value from fewer customers.

New Product Introduction

When a new product is released to the market, there are few competitors and usually few customers. Some potential customers may value your innovation greatly but a lot more customers likely value it much less. This is the stage where you must choose to skim or penetrate the market. To make this decision you need to think ahead to where you think the market is going.

If you have and expect to maintain a monopolistic-type position, like the Apple iPhone, then you probably want to use skim pricing. You don't have to worry about stiff competition for quite a while, so you are able to capture a lot of

Product Life Cycle: Prices Change with Age

value from your customers who like your innovation. You don't have a current competitor forcing you to lower prices, and your expectation is you won't have serious competition for a while.

However, it's rare not to have competitors even in the early stages of a product. In the more common situation where you experience tough competition either at the time of introduction or in the near future, you probably want to use penetration pricing. Your goal is to grow the market rapidly while capturing market share. When the market reaches maturity, it's much harder to increase market share. You need to commit early on to having substantial market share so you can reap the benefits when maturity arrives.

As clearly as possible, describe your eventual product portfolio. What substitutes and complements will you be introducing? Does the price of your new product affect the performance of your overall portfolio down the road? Take this into account as you set your earliest prices. One software startup company I've worked with has launched a line of free products. It's tough to make money on free, but the managers of this company have clearly defined their product roadmap and understand how they will generate revenue from complementary products. This is strategic penetration pricing.

Growth

Growth is the exciting stage. Customer count is growing rapidly, and competitors are entering the market. Your overall pricing strategy is likely to follow from whatever you decided in the introduction phase of the product life cycle.

If you chose a skimming strategy during product introduction, then you will want to begin slowly decreasing prices to make your product affordable to more customers. If you find unexpected fierce competition, you will want to consider switching to a penetration or neutral pricing strategy.

If you entered the market using penetration pricing, then you're probably experiencing increased competition, putting downward pressure on price. If the market is still growing rapidly, you want to continue to price aggressively to increase market share. This is the time to become the dominant player. Although you're focused on the sales (and price) side of your business, you also need to focus on costs. Take full advantage of any learning curve effects. As the growth rate begins to slow down, you'll want to shift to a more neutral pricing strategy where you aren't gaining market share. This is when the longer-term market prices become established, and as much as possible you'd like them to be higher.

Maturity

In this stage, customer growth has essentially stopped. The only new competitors are ones that want to compete on costs and price. Prices are relatively stable at this stage. You should be using a neutral pricing strategy. Avoid competing on price. This will only bring down overall industry profits.

Most companies don't want to stay stagnant, they want to grow. Grow through segmentation. Create new price segmentation mechanisms, but even more important use the versioning and product portfolio techniques discussed in Part Three.

Decline

When a market is in decline, many companies exit. This may open the door to gradual price increases. Sales volumes will decrease faster than any price increases, so revenue and profits will go down. If you remain in the market, look for opportunities to simplify your pricing and raise prices. No need to have complex pricing segmentation strategies for very few customers. If possible, raise prices on new customers only. Remember, customers abhor price increases.

Product Life Cycle: Prices Change with Age

In many cases a product is in decline, but the market is not. This frequently happens when customers buy later generations of the same product. If you offer both generations, then you will want to manage pricing of the entire portfolio.

Portfolio

> The lifeblood of our business is that R&D spend. There's nothing that flows through a pipe or down a wire or anything else. We have to continuously create new innovation that lets people do something they didn't think they could do the day before.
> —Steve Ballmer

#impactpricing

At every stage of a product's life cycle, you also want to clearly understand where that product fits within the product portfolio. Many companies, especially those in high-tech, release generation after generation of product. Each generation has its own life cycle. For example, when Intel released the Pentium chip, they had to decide how to price it relative to the 80486 (the previous generation) that was doing well on the market. Should the Pentium be more expensive because it has more features? Or should it be less expensive so they could move more customers from the 80486 to the new platform?

A common practice in high-tech is to release the new product at the same price as the old one, while lowering the price of the older version. Apple does this frequently, releasing the iPhone 3G at the same price points as the original iPhone, while reducing the price of the original. As a consumer I love this strategy. Prices on products keep coming down. Products keep getting better but don't go up in price. My wallet likes it. However, as a businessman I'm skeptical. There was an obvious market for the older generation at the existing price, and the new product has additional capability. You may try entering with a slightly higher price. It's always easier to lower prices later than to raise them.

IMPACT PRICING

Summary

Product life cycles are predictable. This provides the opportunity to look ahead and decide which pricing strategies make sense today and in the future. It all starts with pricing for new product introductions. How much pricing power do you have? If you own and expect to maintain a monopolistic position then you have a lot of pricing power and should probably skim. If you expect to have strong competitors in the near future, then you have much less pricing power and should probably use penetration prices. The growth stage pricing strategy is usually a continuation of the initial strategy. By the time the market matures, you will want to be at neutral pricing and compete only on segmentation and differentiation but not on price.

The reason for looking at the product life cycle is you can easily look ahead and reason backwards to make better decisions at earlier stages. The same is true for your product portfolio. If you can clearly define your future substitutes and complements, you can use that knowledge to price more appropriately before they are released.

Summary Questions

- ✔ Do you have pricing guidelines in place that change as a product moves through its life cycle?
- ✔ What products are you developing where you could use a skimming strategy?
- ✔ Are you carefully choosing between penetration and skim pricing during new product introduction?

Actions: What are you going to do?

Wrap Up:
Now What?

Benjamin Franklin may have discovered electricity, but it was the man who invented the meter who made the money.

—Earl Wilson

Pricing is a complex topic that could fill a book hundreds if not thousands of pages long. The goal of this book was to focus on the areas of pricing that have an impact.

The single most important concept to take away from Part One is value-based pricing. This is a concept of how to think about pricing. It teaches you how to think about how your customers make choices. Value-based pricing reminds you that value comes from differentiation. Once you internalize this way of thinking, you'll use it to analyze every decision your customers make. It will become second nature. Without this way of thinking it's hard to understand and implement the pricing strategies in the next parts.

IMPACT PRICING

Part Two is where the real impact begins. You already implicitly knew that different customers paid different amounts. You see it when companies have sales or offer coupons. This part gave you a process to understand price segmentation while presenting and explaining numerous examples. Your profitability can be significantly enhanced by searching for and finding new ways to price segment. It's not that hard. Keep trying.

If I had to choose the most important concept in Part Three, it would be versioning. Almost all firms should do this. Versioning uses product features to help segment markets on price. You are certainly aware of it around you, but now you know what to do. Although versioning has the most impact, don't underestimate the power of complementary products.

Without a doubt "customers despise price increases" is the most important concept in Part Four. Most of the strategies presented in this part were methods to avoid raising prices. You often need to think ahead so that actions you take today don't cause unnecessary price increases in the future.

Pricing Drives Products

Pricing is usually an afterthought. Companies have a product ready to go to market and then ask, How much should we charge? "OK" companies have sound pricing processes in place to answer this question. They use value-based pricing and pricing segmentation techniques. These OK companies are more likely to get their pricing right.

"Good" companies move pricing further back into the design cycle. Estimating how much a customer is willing to pay (using value-based pricing, of course) informs the product design team on which features to put in and which ones to leave out. These good companies add value by intentionally adding differentiation. These good companies are more likely to release the right products.

Wrap Up: Now What?

The "better" companies use pricing to determine what products to develop. They think about versioning and complements to design a product portfolio where they can be the most competitive in the customer segments they have targeted. These better companies are more likely to flourish in the market.

"Best" companies, the truly great ones, have figured out how to create a market where they can legitimately skim. There is no competition because what they have developed is so unique. And there won't be competition because they have created differentiation that can't be copied. This is what Warren Buffett meant when he said, "The single most important decision in evaluating a business is pricing power."

What about your company? What pricing processes do you have in place? How does pricing fit into your product development? Do you think about the differentiation of individual products and how that enables you to capture more customer value? Do you think about the product portfolio and how that enables you to capture more industry profit? Do you think about skimming and what it would take to create a product with real pricing power?

Bring pricing into your product development process. Bring it into your product definition process. You'll profit from it.

Is Your Pricing Right?

Every pricing situation is unique, so no book can answer that question for you. Hopefully this book gave you the structure to answer this question yourself.

If someone were to ask you, "Is your pricing right?," an ideal answer to that question would be something like:

Our corporate strategy is _____, and our pricing strategies contribute to achieving it.

IMPACT PRICING

We have fully implemented value-based pricing, and the entire company now thinks in terms of how much value we are delivering to our customers, especially the product development team.

We understand our fixed and variable costs and how they are used in pricing.

We use many pricing segmentation mechanisms, some from all four types. However, we are constantly on the search for more.

We carefully manage our product portfolios. For our substitutes, we make more margin on higher-end products. For our complements we know which products and prices our customers use when choosing us over our competitors.

We're ready for changes in the environment that will cause our prices to change. We have plans in place to handle the next recession, the next time our costs increase, and the next time our competitors' behaviors change.

If you can give an answer like this honestly, then you're far ahead of your competition. None of this is easy, but it is profitable.

A price is just a number. Setting a price is an event in time. Pricing is an ongoing process. Optimal pricing is an ongoing journey.

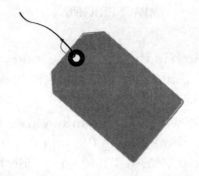

How This Book Was Priced

Toward the end of the book writing process, I asked the marketing team at Entrepreneur Press what price they were planning to use. After all, I'm a pricing expert and thought maybe we should try something interesting.

They told me the book would be priced at $19.95. Most of their books are priced at this level. They have experience with the channel at this price. Everything just flows smoothly.

"Can I change it?" I asked before knowing what I would do. They said, "Sure." ... Now I have to do something.

My initial inclination was to choose a price like $21.87. I liked this price for several reasons. First and foremost, it might grab more attention. I also liked that it was above what the channel (bookstores) expected so we wouldn't be shortchanging them. However, I was a little worried that there might be some odd consumer behavior that $22 might be too high. Since we didn't do any research on the acceptable price points, this decision is coming from experience.

IMPACT PRICING

The marketing team had the experience, and I didn't want to take too big a risk. Since this was my first book, I wanted to rely on the experts.

So I narrowed down the decision to either $19.95 or $20 even. If the experts think this is the proper price range, who am I to say differently? But I had to decide between these two prices. As you know from the cover, I chose $20. The reason has to do with consumer psychology. When consumers see prices like $19.95, they think it's a good deal, and of course this book is a good deal. You will hopefully make thousands of times more in profits implementing ideas from this book than you spent purchasing it. The other reason to price at $19.95 is in case you were choosing between this book and one priced at $30 this book looks like a much better deal. Notice this is a "which one?" type decision.

However, my guess is you made a "Will I?" decision when purchasing this book, not a "Which One?" So the price won't be compared to a competitive book, rather, it would be compared to what you think you should pay, your own reference price. Round prices like $20 look like higher quality, and I wanted to signal to you that this is a quality book so you would set your reference price high.

Unfortunately I'm not able to do interesting pricing segmentation or portfolio pricing strategies. After all it's only my first book. Nor could we test different price points since the price is printed on the cover. So I was only able to select a single price.

That is how this book came to be priced at $20. Now you know a little of what goes through the mind of a pricing strategist.

Glossary

Accessory An add-on item typically sold in addition to a major purchase item. Has little or no value without the major item.

B2B Business-to-business markets.

B2C Business-to-consumer markets.

Bundling Selling two or more items together for a single price.

Captive customers People who have made a main purchase decision that then puts them at the mercy of a single supplier for additional purchases. For example, moviegoers can only purchase popcorn from the theater where they selected to watch the movie.

Channel The series of resellers used to sell products from the manufacturer to the end-user. Also known as a *distribution channel*.

IMPACT PRICING

Choice value The amount of value in dollars a customer places on one product, knowing what the next best alternative choice is.

Complements When the purchase of one product makes the purchase of another product more likely.

Consumable good A type of product that's used up relatively quickly. Typically purchased repeatedly.

Corporate strategy The overall strategy of a company. How the company will achieve its vision.

Cost-plus pricing A pricing tactic that takes the cost of manufacturing a product (usually standard costs) and marks that cost up a specific margin.

Coupons A method of price segmentation where some customers find, clip, carry, and redeem a voucher for a discount. Price-sensitive customers are more likely to use coupons.

Deal value The overall perception of a customer about a purchase decision. Good deal value implies the customer paid a low price for a lot of choice value.

De-bundling Removing a previously bundled feature from a product offering and selling it separately.

Demand curve A graph that shows the quantity of product a company expects to sell at different price points. Typically quantity is on the x-axis (horizontal) and price is on the y-axis (vertical).

Differential pricing Another term for *price segmentation*.

Differentiation How the product under consideration differs from its competition.

Discriminatory pricing Another term for *price segmentation*.

Glossary

Distributors Middlemen in a channel that purchase product from a manufacturer and resell it to another customer.

Durable good A product that lasts a long time.

Dynamic pricing Price segmentation where conditions at the time of the transaction determine the price that is set.

EDLP (every day low pricing) A pricing strategy where companies maintain consistently low prices and don't have frequent sales events. Contrast with *Hi-Lo*.

Elasticity A measure of responsiveness of number of units sold to a change in price. For highly elastic markets, a small change in price causes a large swing in quantity sold.

End-aisle display The display at the end of the aisles in grocery stores or other retailers.

Escalation The act of requesting a lower price from a person within the same company who has more pricing authority. For example, when negotiating to buy a car, the salesperson always has to ask the manager.

Fixed costs Costs that don't change when building the next set of units.

Forward pricing The act of using future costs to determine current prices. The assumption is a very low current price will drive high volume, which will lower manufacturing costs.

Freemium A functional product that's given away for free with the intent of upselling a select set of these customers into paid versions with more features.

Good, Better, Best A common price segmentation method where a company offers three levels of a product. Price-sensitive customers tend to purchase Good, price-insensitive customers tend to purchase best, and uncertain customers tend to purchase Better.

IMPACT PRICING

Hi-Lo A pricing strategy where a company sets relatively high prices and offers frequent and large discounts to attract customers. Contrast with EDLP.

Incremental costs The costs of building the next set of units. Another term for *variable costs*.

Loss leader A product that companies sell below their costs to attract customers with the expectation that they will sell other products at a profit.

Loyal customers Customers who choose to purchase the same product over and over again. They exhibit a strong preference for that product.

Loyalty programs Programs put in place to reward loyal customers. For example, the airlines have frequent flyer programs that reward the best customers.

Marginal costs The cost of building the next set of units. Another term for *variable costs*.

Market cap pricing Pricing with the specific goal of maximizing market capitalization. Most applicable to startups looking for funding.

Market capitalization The overall value of a company. For a public company this is the amount needed to purchase all outstanding shares. For a private company, it's the amount of an investment (recent or future) divided by the percentage of the company being purchased for that investment.

Market segment A categorization of types of businesses. Some examples are automotive, industrial, consumer, medical, and energy. Many companies, especially B2B companies, set different prices for customers based on their market.

Negotiated pricing Transactions where the price is negotiated with the individual customer.

Glossary

Pay-as-you-wish A pricing strategy that lets customers pay whatever they want to pay.

Penetration pricing Setting aggressive prices with the intent of growing market share and/or growing the size of the market.

Perceived value The value from the perspective of the customer.

Perishable good A product or service that becomes worthless at a point in time if not used. For example an airline seat is a perishable good that if not filled has no value once the plane takes off.

Price ending The right-hand digits of a price. For example, 99 cents is a common price ending for lower-priced consumer products.

Price segmentation Selling similar products to different customers at different prices.

Price sensitivity An indicator of willingness to pay. Customers with high price sensitivity have a low willingness to pay.

Price war Two or more companies competing on price. One or more companies lower price to win more market share and other companies lower price to avoid losing share. This can keep going until the last company standing is the one with the lowest costs.

Pricing power The ability to raise prices without hugely impacting demand.

Pricing psychology The study of consumer irrationality in relation to pricing.

Pricing strategy A directive to people who set prices on how they should do their job.

Product funnel The concept to start customers buying relatively inexpensive low-risk products and work them down the funnel to where some are buying more expensive products.

Product life cycle The stages of a product's life, typically driven by changes in competition and demand. The stages are innovation, growth, maturity, and decline.

Product portfolio More than one related product in a product line. They can be complements or substitutes.

Prospect theory A psychological finding where people view losses as much larger than equivalent-sized gains. The saying is "Losses loom larger than gains."

Quantity discount Offering a lower price per unit when higher volumes are purchased.

Real value An objective measure of value. Think of this as the value an unbiased and thorough engineer would place on a product or service.

Reference price The price a potential customer expects to pay for a product.

Regional pricing Price segmentation where companies charge a different price based on geographical location.

Retailers Channel members that sell directly to consumers.

Sensitivity See *price sensitivity*.

Separating pricing mechanism The method in price segmentation used to keep people with high willingness to pay from being able to purchase at the lower price.

Signaling (price as a signal of quality) Customers commonly infer higher quality for products with higher prices.

Skimming A pricing strategy to charge higher than "normal" prices due to a monopolistic position with the intent of lowering prices later to capture more customers.

Glossary

Standard cost A cost calculated by summing all the manufacturing overhead and variable costs and dividing that number by the number of units produced.

Step pricing A pricing strategy where a potential high-volume customer will pay higher prices for the earliest units until they take delivery on an agreed-on high volume. Then future units are sold at a lower price.

Strategy A description of how to achieve a set of goals.

Substitute Two products are substitutes when the act of purchasing one product makes it less likely that the same customer will purchase the other.

TIOLI (take it or leave it) A type of market (or pricing strategy) where the seller sets a price and the potential customer simply chooses to purchase or not. There is no negotiation.

Unbundling Same as *de-bundling*.

Utility theory An economic theory where all people make decisions based on their own perceived best interest.

Value An ambiguous word. See *value in use, choice value, deal value, real value*, and *perceived value*.

Value accounting A process used to estimate a customer's willingness to pay.

Value-based pricing A way to think about pricing where the prices are set to capture customers' willingness to pay.

Value in use The value a customer receives from using a product. If measured in dollars this value must exceed the price for a purchase to occur.

Variable costs The cost of building the next set of units.

Versioning A price segmentation method based on creating different versions of products targeted at different customers who are willing to pay different amounts.

IMPACT PRICING

Vision A picture of what the company may look like many years in the future.

Volume discount See *quantity discount*.

"Which one?" A question customers usually have to answer when making a purchase decision. Used as a simple reminder that customers make choices between products in a category. See also *"Will I?"*.

"Will I?" A question customers always have to answer when making a purchase decision. "Will I purchase a product in this category?" Used as an easy reminder that customers have to value the use of the product higher than the price before purchasing. See also *"Which one?"*.

Willingness to pay The maximum price a customer will pay for a product.

Yield pricing A pricing strategy where companies price perishable goods dynamically based on current levels of demand and the time remaining until the good perishes. Commonly used in pricing airline seats and hotel rooms.

Bibliography

Anderson, Chris. *Free: The Future of a Radical Price.* Hyperion, 2009.

Hart, Rupert M. *Resisting Pricing Pressure in Recession & Recovery.* RecessionStormingMedia, 2009.

Holden, Reed, and Mark Burton. *Pricing with Confidence: 10 Ways to Stop Leaving Money on the Table.* John Wiley & Sons, 2008.

Kahneman, Daniel, and Amos Tversky. *Choices, Values, and Frames.* Cambridge University Press, 2000.

Nagle, Thomas T., John E. Hogan, and Joseph Zale. *The Strategy and Tactics of Pricing: A Guide to Growing More Profitably,* 5th Ed. Prentice Hall, 2010.

Raju, Jagmohan, and Z. John Zhang. *Smart Pricing: How Google, Priceline, and Leading Businesses Use Pricing Innovation for Profitability.* Wharton School Publishing, 2010.

Index

index

Index

A
Accessories, 128
Add-on items, 126–127
Ad-supported business, 138
Age, segmentation by, 88
Airlines
   baggage fees, 46, 60, 84
   cost increases, 72
   de-bundling by, 130, 154
   price segmentation, 80, 84, 97, 158
   price wars, 158, 161
   product versioning, 117, 118, 123
Amazon, 79
American Airlines, 161
Apple
   broken promises blog, 59
   corporate strategy, 4, 5
   iPad pricing, 32, 122
   iPhone pricing, 19–20, 167
   iTunes apps, 137
   perceived product value, 29–30
Aspirin analogy, 35
Attorneys, 61
Automatic markdowns, 147–148
Average selling price, 7

B
B2B markets
   escalations, 147
   geographic segmentation, 87, 89
   learning competitors' prices, 46–47
   negotiated vs. TIOLI pricing, 23
   purchase behavior segmentation, 89–90, 96, 105
   variable costs and, 68–69
   versioning in, 119–120
B2C markets, 23
Baggage fees, 46, 60, 84

Index

"Bags Fly Free" campaign, 60
Barnes and Noble, 97
Basic products, 116–117
Beetle pricing, 20
Ben and Jerry's, 10, 11
Best Buy, 128
Bicycle shops, 120–121
Blueskylocal.com, 104
BMW, 4
Book pricing, 172–173
Brands, 48, 56–58
Broad, Eli, 54
Broken promises, 59
Brooks Brothers, 95–96, 148
Buffett, Warren, 171
Bundling, 130–131
Burger King, 115, 116–117
Business travelers, 123, 158, 161
Buy.com, 146
Buying decisions. *See also* Perceived value
   customer perceptions and, 28–33, 38–39
   impact of economic changes on, 152–155
   products and choices, 33–38, 174
   value accounting, 42–45
   value-based, 38–39

C

Cable TV companies, 105
Captive customers, 128–129
Car buyers, 90
Carports, 54–55
"Cascade of Broken Promises," 59
Chick-Fil-A, 10, 11
Chief executive officers (CEOs), 4, 6–7, 10

Chinese companies, 161
Choice value, 31
Coca-Cola, 48, 103–104
Community organizations, 95
Community service strategies, 10–11
Comparisons. *See also* Buying decisions; Perceived value
   choice value, 31
   differing standards, 38–39
   influencing, 59–60
   seeking information about, 45
Competing products
   choice value vs., 31
   customer awareness, 45
   influencing perceived price, 60
   limited during new product stage, 164–165
   in value accounting calculations, 45–51
Competitive advantage, 4, 11
Competitors' prices
   as factor in value-based pricing, 28–29, 157
   influencing customer perceptions, 60
   responding to changes, 157–161
   as starting point for pricing, 42–43
   in value accounting calculations, 45–51
   volume discounts, 102
Complementary products
   accessories, 128
   bundling and de-bundling, 129–131
   captive customers and, 128–129

Index

defined, 114, 125
durables and consumables, 127–128
free versions as, 138
loss leaders, 126–127
product funnel, 132
Comstrat, 49
Conjoint analysis, 49
Consultant costs, 71
Consumable products, 127–128
Corporate strategies. *See also* Pricing strategies
   basic pricing approaches and, 21
   low-price leadership, 11–13, 148, 149
   nonfinancial, 10–11
   relation to vision, 4–6
Cost-plus pricing, 21–22, 73–74
Costs
   fixed, 66–68
   importance in low-price approach, 13, 149
   inflation's impact, 153–155
   price wars' impact, 160–161
   standard, 70–72
   variable, 68–70
Coupons, 94–95, 152
Croton watches, 146
Customer behavior. *See also* Buying decisions
   impact of economic changes, 152–155
   price segmentation by, 93–98, 105
Customer characteristics, segmentation by, 87–90
Customer loyalty, 97, 107–108

Customer perceptions
   choice and in-use value, 31–33
   creating, 56–62
   elements of, 28–31
   of fair pricing, 82–84
   of price increases, 144–145, 170
   second-best options, 45–51
   seeking information about, 44, 45, 56, 58
Customer types. *See also* Price segmentation
Customer types, value accounting and, 44

D

Databases, 47
De-bundling, 129–130, 154
Decision items
   creating captive customers with, 129
   defined, 126–127
   giving away, 127–128
   unbundling, 130
Decline stage, product life cycle, 166–167
Dell, 23
Demand curves, 69
Development costs, 66, 67–68
Differentiation
   to blunt price competition, 158, 161
   brands, 48
   estimating dollar value, 49–50
   role in creating perceived value, 30, 54–58
Discounts
   age-based, 82, 88
   asking for, 99

Index

Discounts (*continued*)
   first-time buyer, 104–105
   with high initial prices, 145–148
   volume purchase, 102–103
   weather-related, 103–104
Discount stores, 12–13
Disneyland, 88
Dupuit, Jules, 117
Durable products, 127–128
DVDs, 131
Dynamic pricing, 143

E
Early adopters, 19–20
eBay, 128
Economic changes, 151–155
Elasticity, 37–38
Electronic Arts, 67–68
Employees, sharing strategy with, 4–5
Encryption software, 123
End-aisle displays, 96
End-of-life products, 20
Entrepreneurial startups, 7–9
Escalations, 147
Every Day Low Price strategy, 148–149
Express Mail, 58–59

F
Facebook, 137
Fairness, 73, 82–84
Filene's Basement, 147–148
First-class air travel, 117, 161
First-time buyer discounts, 104–105
Fixed costs, 66–68, 70–71
Folgers coffee, 57–58
Forward pricing, 9, 19
Freemiums, 137–138
Free products, 135–139

Freeware authors, 98
Fuel prices, 72, 154
Fuel surcharges, 154

G
Garbage collection, 104, 108
Generic products, 118
Geographic segmentation, 87, 89
Gerstner, Lew, 4
Gillette, 127
Goals for pricing strategies, 3–4
Godin, Seth, 59
Good-better-best pricing, 121–122
Google, 66, 138
Grocery stores
   complementary products, 126
   end-aisle displays, 96
   neutral pricing, 18
   versioning in, 118
Gross profit, 70. *See also* Profit margins
Growth markets, 160
Growth stage, product life cycle, 165–166

H
Hi-Lo strategy, 148–149
Historical purchase behavior, 89–90
Hotwire, 97
HP, 127
Hype, 62

I
IBM, 4
Ikea, 4
Inertia, loyalty vs., 108
Inflation, 153–155
Infomercials, 130

Index

Information, free, 136–137
Ink, 127–128
Intel, 23, 118–119, 167
Internet companies, 8
Internet segmentation strategies, 97–98
In-use value, 31–32
Investors, 9
iPads, 32, 122
iPhone pricing, 19–20, 167
ITunes apps, 137

J
JC Penney, 148
Jobs, Steve, 57

K
Kmart, 12, 13

L
LaCroix, Darren, 139
Lake Tahoe resorts, 97
Leisure travelers, 123
Life cycles of products, 163–167
LinkedIn, 137–138
Local pricing, 88–89
Loss leaders, 126–127
Low-price strategies, 11–13, 148–149
Loyalty clubs, 97, 108

M
Macintosh computers, 29–30
Macy's, 148
Madden NFL '11 game, 67–68
Manufacturing overhead, 70–71
Margins, 73
Market cap pricing strategies, 6–10
Market growth, price wars with, 160

Marketing, 29, 30–31, 56–58
Market segments, 89, 122–123. *See also* Price segmentation
Market share, efforts to increase, 159, 160
Matinee pricing, 104
Maturity stage, product life cycle, 166
McDonald's
  complementary products, 114
  loss leaders, 127
  meal deals, 131
  senior citizen discounts, 88
Meal deals, 131
"Meaningful Brands from Meaningless Differentiation," 57
Mercedes, 4
Microsoft, 128
Migration Assistant, 59
Milk prices, 126
Monopolies, 34
Movie theaters, 82, 119, 128–129

N
Negotiated pricing. *See also* B2B markets
  escalations, 147
  take-it-or-leave-it vs., 22–24, 66
  variable costs and, 68–69
  versioning with, 119–120
Netflix, 145
Network membership, free, 137
Neutral pricing, 18, 164, 166
Newegg, 146
New markets, 19, 160
New products. *See also* Product development

Index

New products (*continued*)
  impact of price on buying decisions, 34–35
  product life cycle stage, 164–165
  as response to inflation, 154
  skimming on, 19–20, 145–146, 164–165
  value in use, 32
Nonfinancial objectives, 10–11
Nordstrom, 148

O

Objectives, 3–4, 10–11
Observable costs, 72
Outlet malls, 104
Overall value, 33
Overhead costs, 70–71

P

Packaged foods, 153–154
Pay-as-you-wish methods, 98
Penetration pricing
  as new-product strategy, 165, 166
  overview, 18–19, 164
Pentium chips, 167
Perceived value
  choice and in-use, 31–33
  elements of, 28–31
  estimating, 42–45
  increasing, 56–62
Playstation, 128
Podcasters, 98
Point-of-purchase segmentation methods, 101–105
Popcorn, 128–129
Portfolio pricing, 167
Positioning, 11–13
Price buyers, 90
Price elasticity, 37–38
Price increases, 144–145, 170
Priceline, 97
Price segmentation
  benefits, 80–81, 170
  by customer behavior, 93–98, 147
  customer characteristics for, 87–90
  customer loyalty and, 97, 107–108
  during economic downturns, 152
  fairness, 82–84
  point-of-purchase methods, 101–105
  as primary growth strategy, 166
  in response to competitor price changes, 158
  steps in, 81–82
  versioning compared, 115
Price sensitivity, 93–98, 144–145
Price wars, 18–19, 159–161
Pricing strategies. *See also* Value-based pricing
  EDLP vs. Hi-Lo, 148–149
  evaluating, 171–172
  low-price leadership, 11–13, 148, 149
  market cap approach, 6–10
  negotiated vs. TIOLI, 22–24
  objectives, 3–4
  overview of basic approaches, 18–21
  as part of product development, 170–171
  during product life cycle, 163–167
  relation to corporate objectives, 5–6, 21
  responsibility for, 6

Index

value-based concept, 21–22
Pricing with Confidence (Reed/Burton), 120
Printers and ink, 127–128
Product advantages and disadvantages, 47–50
Product development. *See also* New products
  costs excluded from pricing, 66, 67–68
  as response to inflation, 154
  role of pricing in, 170–171
  versioning in, 114–121
Product funnel, 132
Product life cycles, 163–167
Product portfolios, 167
Products, free, 135–139
Profit margins
  calculating, 70
  importance to investors, 9
  strategies to increase, 7, 160–161
  value-based pricing advantages, 22, 73–74
  with versioning, 116–117
Promises, broken, 59
Promotion. *See* Marketing
Public radio, 98
Purchasing decisions. *See* Buying decisions

Q

Quality
  pricing as indicator, 60–62, 146
  versioning based on, 121–122
Quarter-end discounts, 96, 147

R

Radiohead, 98
Razors, 127
Real value, 29–31
Rebates, 95
Recessions, 152–153
Reference prices, 33, 146
Resale data, 89–90

S

Sales events, 95–96
Sales force product knowledge, 57
Sales funnel, 132
Sales tax, 46
Samples, free, 136
San Francisco Giants, 104, 119
Satellite TV companies, 105
Schultz, Howard, 55
Sears, 121
Second-best options, 45–51, 58–60
Segmentation. *See* Price segmentation
Semiconductors, 119
Senior citizen discounts, 88
Separating mechanisms, 81–82
Shark Tank, 7–8
Shipping costs, 46
Simon, Kucher and Partners, 49
Skimming
  defined, 19–20, 164
  as new-product strategy, 145–146, 164–165
Ski resorts, 97
Small business pricing approach, 9–10
Socially conscious objectives, 10–11
Software
  as consumables, 128
  free versions, 137

Index

Software (*continued*)
  pay-as-you-wish model, 98
  product versioning, 123
Sommeliers, 61
Sony, 128
Southwest Airlines, 60, 158
Standard costs, 70–72
Standards of Identity for
  Distilled Spirits (U.S.), 48
Starbucks, 55
Startup companies, 7–9
Stock prices, 6–7
Store brands, 38, 118
Strategies. *See* Corporate
  strategies
Student discounts, 82
Substitutes, 114, 138
Subway, 152–153
Sunk costs, 67
Surcharges, 154

T
Taj Mahal, 88
Take-it-or-leave-it pricing
  negotiated vs., 22–24, 66
  variable costs and, 69–70
Target, 12–13
Temporary pricing, 153
Time-of-day pricing, 104
Trial versions, 138–139
TV pricing, 128
Twitter, 137

U
Unbundling, 130, 154
U.S. Postal Service, 58–59

V
Value accounting
  overview, 42–45
  steps, 45–51
Value-based buying decisions,
  38–39

Value-based pricing
  customer perceptions and,
    28–33
  as optimal approach, 21–22,
    169
  relevance of costs in, 66–70
  value accounting, 42–51
Value buyers, 90
Value creation, 30, 54–58
Value in use, 31–32, 34
Variable costs, 68–70, 71–72,
  153–154
Versioning
  by adding features, 116–121
  basic principles, 114–116,
    170
  by market, 122–123
  quality-based, 121–122
Video games, 128
Vision, 4–6
Vitamin analogy, 35
Vodkas, 48
Volkswagen, 20
Volume discounts, 102–103

W
The Wall Street Journal, 137
Walmart, 5, 11–13, 148
Weak complements, 131
Weather, discounts for,
  103–104
Which one? decisions, 35–38,
  173
Whole Foods, 60
Will I? decisions, 34–35, 173
Wine quality, 61
Wozniak, Steve, 57

X
Xbox, 128

Y
Year-end discounts, 147

About the Author

Mark Stiving, MBA, Ph.D. helps companies implement value-based pricing strategies to increase profit.

As a pricing strategist, he "spreads the gospel" of value-based pricing. His message inspires manufacturers, marketers, and others concerned with pricing to capture greater value through pricing improvements and to focus on creating real, quantifiable value for the benefit of customers and the bottom line.

Mark has addressed pricing professionals and executives at major conferences for the Professional Pricing Society, International Quality and Productivity Center (IQPC), American Marketing Association, Consumer Electronics Design and Installation Association (CEDIA), Marketing Science, and in additional professional settings.

As a coach, Mark helps companies create and implement new pricing strategies to capture more of the value they create. He has consulted with Cisco, Procter and Gamble, Grimes Aerospace, Rogers Corporation, and many small businesses and entrepreneurial ventures. He currently works full time developing and implementing new pricing strategies at National Semiconductor.

Mark has published pricing articles in the *Journal of Consumer Research*, *Management Science*, and the *Journal of Commerce*. He freely shares his knowledge and latest thoughts on pricing at www.PragmaticPricing.com.

As an award-winning speaker, Mark's favorite hobby is public speaking, generously giving back to the Toastmasters community that helped him excel as a professional communicator.

Mark earned a BSEE at The Ohio State University, an MBA at Santa Clara University, and a Ph.D. in Marketing at U.C. Berkeley.